INSIDE ORGANIZATIONS

SAGE was founded in 1965 by Sara Miller McCune to support the dissemination of usable knowledge by publishing innovative and high-quality research and teaching content. Today, we publish over 900 journals, including those of more than 400 learned societies, more than 800 new books per year, and a growing range of library products including archives, data, case studies, reports, and video. SAGE remains majority-owned by our founder, and after Sara's lifetime will become owned by a charitable trust that secures our continued independence.

Los Angeles | London | New Delhi | Singapore | Washington DC | Melbourne

DAVID COGHLAN

INSIDE ORGANIZATIONS

EXPLORING ORGANIZATIONAL EXPERIENCES

Los Angeles | London | New Delhi
Singapore | Washington DC | Melbourne

Los Angeles | London | New Delhi
Singapore | Washington DC | Melbourne

SAGE Publications Ltd
1 Oliver's Yard
55 City Road
London EC1Y 1SP

SAGE Publications Inc.
2455 Teller Road
Thousand Oaks, California 91320

SAGE Publications India Pvt Ltd
B 1/I 1 Mohan Cooperative Industrial Area
Mathura Road
New Delhi 110 044

SAGE Publications Asia-Pacific Pte Ltd
3 Church Street
#10-04 Samsung Hub
Singapore 049483

Editor: Kirsty Smy / Delia Martinez-Alfonso
Editorial assistant: Lyndsay Aitken
Production editor: Sarah Cooke
Copyeditor: Gemma Marren
Proofreader: Neil Dowden
Marketing manager: Sally Ransom
Cover design: Shaun Mercier
Typeset by: C&M Digitals (P) Ltd, Chennai, India
Printed and bound by CPI Group (UK) Ltd,
Croydon, CR0 4YY

Library of Congress Control Number: 2016931724

British Library Cataloguing in Publication data

A catalogue record for this book is available from the British Library

ISBN 978-1-47396-898-1
ISBN 978-1-47396-899-8 (pbk)

At SAGE we take sustainability seriously. Most of our products are printed in the UK using FSC papers and boards. When we print overseas we ensure sustainable papers are used as measured by the PREPS grading system. We undertake an annual audit to monitor our sustainability.

CONTENTS

ABOUT THE AUTHOR

David Coghlan is Professor Emeritus at Trinity Business School, Trinity College Dublin, Ireland and is Fellow Emeritus of the college. He specializes in organization development and action research, and is active in both communities internationally. He has published over 140 articles and book chapters. He is co-author of the internationally popular *Doing Action Research in Your Own Organization* (4th edn, SAGE, 2014) and is co-editor of *The SAGE Encyclopedia of Action Research* (2014). Other books include *Organizational Change and Strategy: An Interlevel Dynamics Approach* (2nd edn, Routledge, 2016). He is co-editor of the four volume sets *Fundamentals of Organization Development* (SAGE, 2010) and *Action Research in Business and Management* (SAGE, 2016). He is currently on the editorial boards of *Journal of Applied Behavioral Science*, *Action Research* and *Action Learning: Research and Practice* among others.

ACKNOWLEDGEMENTS

I owe the foundations of my curiosity about what goes on in organizations to Ed Schein. He introduced me to the work of Erving Goffman, to Don Schon and to the habit of attending to process. For sixty years he has creatively and systematically shaped theory and practice on organizational dynamics by providing rich theoretical and practical reflections on the cultural dynamics of complex systems, process interventions and the clinical research paradigm. As my former teacher and mentor and then my friend, he has shaped my formation and my scholarship. His influence permeates this book.

My immeasurable thanks goes to successive cohorts of the final-year undergraduate course Exploring Organizational Experiences in the Trinity Business School, where their engagement in insider inquiry provided the stimulus for the book and test runs of the chapters as course working papers. Without these students' struggles to master insider inquiry and my effort to accompany them this book would not exist.

I am grateful to David Tuohy and Ann Donohue who provided detailed feedback on each chapter and who challenged me to sharpen my thinking and forms of presentation.

The book has been richly enhanced by the skilled illustrations by Daniel Daly (http://dansdoodles.org). Thank you, Dan, for sharing your skills and your time so generously.

Finally, I acknowledge invaluable help and support of the SAGE editorial and production teams, especially Kirsty Smy, Lyndsay Aitken, Sarah Cooke and Gemma Marren.

INTRODUCTION

It is now commonplace in business undergraduate programmes that students spend time on placements or internships in organizations where they learn the 'real life' of organizations to complement their book learning. In their book learning students gain a great deal of insights into organizations indirectly, i.e. through case studies and their reading. Having direct experience of organizations, however, provides access to the reality of organizations with all their paradoxes and problems, and a challenge to learn through experience rather than from a textbook.

Developing an inquiring attentiveness to organizational processes as they are being experienced is a core skill for undergraduate business students to learn as they move from college into the world of work. It might be expected that efforts to develop a perspective on inquiring into organizational experience would be difficult and troublesome in educational environments where students are encouraged to analyse organizations from a distance and in terms of a priori categories. Such efforts, in fact, challenge students to think differently, not only about their external environment but also about themselves.

Inside Organizations: Exploring Organizational Experiences explores studying organizations from the inside for an undergraduate readership that spends time on placements or internships. It is what is referred to as 'inquiry from the inside', as being 'backstage' or as being immersed in the 'swampy lowlands'. For students working in organizations, attention to what goes on around them evokes questions about how organizations function and sets the foundations for learning.

This is essentially a book about studying organizations. Its theoretical base is in the fields of organizational behaviour, organizational theory, strategy and change from the perspective of being experienced directly. It draws on philosophy, the symbolic and constructivist perspective of organizations, experiential learning, action learning, action science and organization development. The assumption is that experience and inquiry from the perspective of being insiders creates the potential of developing critical thinking skills that students can draw on in their future careers. Its primary aim is to provide a text to accompany undergraduate students whose programmes require a reflective engagement on their experiences in a placement or internship. It is useful for both the students and their supervisors and mentors. Other readers, such as those engaging in insider research at postgraduate level, may find it useful even if it is not specifically directed at them

STRUCTURE OF THE BOOK

There are eight chapters and four appendices. Chapter 1 introduces the notion of studying organizations from the inside. It draws on the notion of organizations as social constructions and introduces the dramatic and symbolic pattern of experience. The emphasis is on a theory of action, that is, what actually takes place, as contrasted with an espoused theory in order to ground understanding of organizational behaviour from insider experience. Chapter 2 introduces the underlying method for inquiring from the inside that enables readers to attend to their experience, be able to question and to formulate and test understanding of what is taking place and to be critical of their own thinking processes. Chapter 3 invites readers to reflect on how they may learn about themselves from working in an organization. Chapter 4 introduces an organizational framework of four levels of behaviour that may be experienced directly by insiders. Chapter 5 discusses some organizational phenomena that insiders experience and witness, such as emotion, rumour/gossip, emotional labour and demotivation and invites readers to reflect critically on episodes of these phenomena and their impact. Chapter 6 invites reflection on the insider's experience of an organization's strategy-in-use. Chapter 7 takes up the processes of organizational learning and change. There are reflective exercises, called *Reflective Pauses*, dotted through each chapter, which invite readers to pause for reflection and apply what they are reading to their own experience in the organization in which they are an intern or on placement. These *Reflective Pauses* feed into and are fed from their learning journal and contribute to their reflective essay. The four appendices provide essential supplementary material and deal respectively with: keeping a learning journal, writing a reflective essay, a guide for supervisors and mentors and, finally, insider inquiry as research. References and further reading are supplied for each chapter at the end of the book.

The emphasis in this book is on students being attentive to what goes on around them, noticing what people say and do, developing a spirit of curiosity and inquiring, and seeking answers to questions while also attending to their own cognitive and learning processes.

1

BEING INSIDE ORGANIZATIONS

> Picture a typical day in your organization. You are doing your work, whatever
> that may be - sitting at a desk working at a computer or on your feet serving
> customers. You observe what is going on around you and you hear what your
> colleagues say to one another as they engage in the work and in casual chitchat.
> Does anything puzzle you about what is going on? Do you notice when there seem
> to be contradictions between what is said and what is done? Does it seem to you
> that a problem was being sidestepped by how a manager responded to a query?
> Do you think that an individual is bullying in his/her manner and getting away
> with it? Do you catch yourself warning yourself to be careful and to tread softly?
> Are there times when your puzzlement is accentuated and you scratch your head
> asking yourself 'What is going on here'?

Welcome to your organization and, more particularly, welcome to your quest to understand it from the perspective of being an insider, that is someone who works in the
organization in whatever capacity. You can learn a lot about an organization by being
observant as you hang around and work in it. Because you are inside and interacting with
work colleagues, both formally on the jobs you have to do and informally in coffee and
lunch breaks, you can develop a theory of the organization that may be hard to put into
words. You see things happening. You hear how these events are interpreted. You may see
formal rules and procedures being enforced on some occasions and on other occasions
being ignored. You have direct experience of managerial behaviour that you may judge
to be effective, or perhaps ineffective. You may experience a dissonance between what
the organization espouses and what it actually does. For yourself, you have expectations

and hopes about how you want to learn to perform and to get on with your bosses and fellow employees. You may have future career ambitions in this organization or you may be using the organization for your own short-term ends. Whatever way you approach your engagement you have to learn the world of the organization, its language and its symbols, and try to fit in and be productive. When you enter a new situation you do so with an expectation of what you expect to occur. You must learn to recognize the behaviour of others as recognizable or meaningful. You need to be able to understand the continuing conversation and actions that unfold in the situation so that changing expectations, perspectives and other circumstantial contingencies can be met and managed.

This chapter introduces the foundations on which the approaches to inquiring from the inside are constructed. The premise that underpins these foundations is that organizations are adaptive coping systems of acquiring, interpreting and applying information and that these activities are founded on shared meanings, many of which are implicit or covert and not easy to uncover. Actions and their accompanying meanings are the focus of this book's approach. The chapter is structured as follows. First, the notion of a theory of action that shapes organizational thinking and behaving is introduced. Second, the notion that organizations are social constructions created by meaning and held together by cultural rules is described. Third, the dramatic or dramaturgic approach focuses on organizing as unfolding practical and symbolic actions, with implications for how the self engages in roles. Fourth, the notion of being backstage provides a central dramaturgical image for insiders to observe and question the relationship between the formal and informal organization.

THEORY OF ACTION

When you think about a situation, what you want to achieve in that situation, and then take some action to bring it about, then you have a theory of action. A theory of action is based on causal thinking that has three components: 1) in situation X, 2) do A, 3) in order to achieve goal B. You typically (as we all do) engage in doing what you intend without putting much thought into how it is that you understand what you are doing. It is when the actual outcome is different from what you intended that a question arises. You have probably said to someone at some point, 'What on earth were you thinking of when you did ...?' You may even have had it said to you. Such a question is challenging you to think about your intentions and is a way of uncovering your theory of action.

Theories of action are rationales in your head that guide behaviour and help to you to make sense of others' behaviours. Two types of theory of action may be distinguished. One is the type that is espoused and which is expressed when you say what you are intending to achieve. This is called *espoused theory*. The second is *theory-in-use*, the theory that is actually employed, frequently tacitly and unbeknownst to you as you employ it. You have tacit mental maps with regard to how to act in situations. This involves the way you plan, implement and review your actions. It is these mental maps that guide your actions rather than the rationales that you explicitly espouse. Generally you are unaware of the maps or theories you use. One way of making sense of this is to say that there is a split between theory and action.

To access your *theory-in-use* you need to look to three elements: the assumptions or conditions that direct behaviour or action, the strategies, plans and actions used to enact the assumptions or governing values and the consequences, i.e. what happens as a result of the action (Figure 1.1). Consequences can be both intended and unintended. Where the consequences of the strategy that is used are what you intended, then your *theory-in-use* is confirmed. This is because there is a match between intention and outcome. However, there may be a mismatch between intention and outcome. In other words, the consequences may be unintended. While I develop further elements of theory of action in other chapters to explore what actually goes on in the organization, here it is important try to become aware of the notion of a theory of action and to begin to uncover your theories of action. Then you can begin to ask questions as you look at what people actually do and ask yourself what these actions mean in what they achieve, whether intended or not.

Figure 1.1   Theory of action

ORGANIZATIONS AS SOCIAL CONSTRUCTIONS

Organizations are understood to be social constructions. This means that they are arte-facts created by human beings to serve their ends. They follow processes that are shaped by human purposes and they do not exist independently of human minds and actions. They are systems of human action in which means and ends are guided by intentions, strategies and hoped-for outcomes. They are, in effect, created by meaning, with a rich tapestry of cultural rules, roles and interactions.

You live in a world mediated by meaning. Indeed, meaning is at the heart of human living. Meaning is understood as being constructed and maintained through social inter-action; therefore, the source of meaning is intrinsically social. Social interaction is the process that *forms* human conduct, instead of being merely a means or setting for the expression or release of human conduct. As such, meaning itself is fragile because, as well as truth, there is error. There is fiction as well as fact, deceit as well as honesty, myth as well as science.

Meaning performs a number of important functions. It performs a cognitive function whereby you engage in acts of understanding in how you understand what events might mean. It performs an affective function whereby you have feelings and emotions about what events might mean. It performs an effective function whereby there is the world that you make through your intentions, your planning, your enacting and your evaluat-ing. Meaning is not a simple matter, as several levels of meaning may exist in a given experience. At any one time, you may be concerned only with a single meaning in a given situation; other meanings may be ignored or left for later reflection.

Meanings are communicated through words and gestures. Any word or gesture may signify what the person who is making the gesture intends to communicate, what the person to whom the gesture is directed receives and the joint action that is to arise by the articulation of the acts of both. Any gesture has meaning not only for the person who makes it but also for the person who receives it. When the meanings of both the recipi-ent and the sender are in alignment, they understand each other. When they are not in alignment there is confusion, communication is ineffective, interaction is impeded and joint action is blocked.

The field of organizations hangs on meaning. Organizations and communities are developed through acts of meaning. They are held together by common fields of experi-ence, common modes of understanding, common measures of judgement and common consent. There are many carriers of meaning: language, symbols, art, shared assump-tions, spontaneous intersubjectivity and the lives and actions of people, to cite the more important ones. Understanding organizational actions requires inquiry into the con-structions of meaning that individuals make about themselves, their situation and the world, and how their actions may be driven by assumptions and compulsions as well as by values.

Metaphors and imagery play a role in capturing how you may think about organizations as social constructions. For example, Morgan's book *Images of Organization*, which offers views of an organization as a machine, an organism, a brain, a culture, a political system and a psychic prison, may provoke you to think laterally, rather than in mechanistic terms. Bolman and Deal in *Reframing Organizations* present a four lenses framework: structural, human resource, political and symbolic ways of viewing and understanding organizations. Each of these is bringing a particular meaning to understanding organizations. These and others enable you both to be creative in how you seek to capture how you might understand an organization and to have an insight into how you may understand your organization as a social construction.

THE ORGANIZATION AS A LILY POND

It can be said that organizations lead two lives – a formal and informal life. The formal life is characterized by what is essentially its official information. This comprises statements about its mission, its context, markets or service environment, its strategies and goals and reports on its performance (as in an annual report). Within an organization there is information about its management structure, management policies, human resource policies about duties and responsibilities, sick leave, holiday entitlements and benefits. There are policies about bullying, harassment, equal opportunities and so on. These are artefacts that express an organization's formal life that is accessible through documentation.

There is also the informal life of an organization, which is the organization as it is experienced, and which can only be known by being an insider. Here you find the organizational underworld, characterized by assumptions, cultural rules, emotions, attitudes and relationships. While the formal organization acts on the implicit assumption that the only emotions that exist in the organization are goodwill based on satisfaction, motivation and energetic commitment towards the organization's goals, experience shows that organizations are more complex than that. Organizations are full of emotions: ambition, jealousy, envy, anger, frustration, hate, alienation, demotivation, love, friendship, enthusiasm and so on. Experiences of working in an organization may form attitudes that it is a nice place to work or that it is not a nice place to work. It may be that individuals perceive membership of the organization as providing a solid career path or not. Work relationships may be fraught with jealousy and contaminated by naked ambition and back-stabbing, resulting in low trust and minimal cooperation. Cliques may dominate participation and control communication. Knowledge of what is going on may be largely based on rumour and gossip and false positivity. There may be cultural assumptions that mean that whatever changes are made things remain the same.

These two lives of an organization are often portrayed as an iceberg. The formal life captured by what is seen above the water line and the informal life by what is hidden and below the water line. You know that the vast bulk of an iceberg is actually hidden below the water. So it is with the informal organization. Schein critiques the iceberg metaphor as presenting the informal organization as frozen and static. He suggests the alternative image of the lily pond. The flowers and leaves that you see on the water are the visible artefacts. What is below the waterline is not a frozen mass, but rather a vibrant dynamic ecosystem as the roots are fed by the nutrients to create and nourish the flowers and the leaves that come to the surface. So it is that the cultural rules and meanings as played out under the surface are what drive the visible actions of organizations. In your insider inquiry you are asking questions about the behaviour that you see and hear and what such behaviour means, for the individuals involved and for the organization. You may also have a felt sense that there is more than meets the eye, that is what is hidden below the surface that is not visible, and you try to understand what that is and how it contributes to what is on the surface. In other words you are searching for your organization's theory of action.

Now I invite you take a reflective pause in which you are invited to apply what you are reading in this chapter to your experience in your organization.

REFLECTIVE PAUSE

Think of an incident in your organization:

- Who said what to whom? How did that person react? What happened then?
- Does this incident fit a pattern (previous incidents ...)?
- How did you have access to this incident?
- What do you know about it and what do you not know about it?
- What might it tell you about the organization?

ORGANIZATIONAL CULTURE

A significant construct for exploring the hidden life of organizations is that of organizational culture. Edgar Schein presents organizational culture in terms of shared assumptions that a given organization has learned as it solved its problems of external adaptation and internal integration and that worked well enough to be considered valid and, therefore, to be taught to new members as the correct way to perceive, think and feel in relation to these problems. He describes three levels of culture which go from the visible to the invisible or tacit. The first level is the artefact level. These are the visible things - what you see, hear and feel as you work in the organization - the visible layout of the office, whether people work with their door open or closed, how people are dressed, how people treat one another, how meetings are conducted, how disagreements or conflicts are handled and so on. The difficulty about these visible artefacts is that they are hard to decipher. You don't know why people behave this way or why things are this way. They often don't know either. When you ask these questions you get the official answers, the espoused values that the organization wants to present. This is the second level of culture – organizational values. Open doors are a sign of open communication and teamwork, first-name greetings are a sign of informality – sort of thing. Yet you know that this is not always true, that organizations, not unlike individuals, do not always live up to what they espouse, not necessarily due to any deliberate, nefarious or conspiratorial reasons to deceive but for complex, unknown, hidden reasons. A more common answer to your question is likely to be, 'I don't know; they did things this way long before I joined and I got the message early on that this is how we do things here'. So you come to the third level of culture, that of shared tacit assumptions. These are the taken-for-granted assumptions, its theory of action, which have grown up in the organization and which have made it successful.

Culture is embedded in the experience of a given group. You can't have culture on your own. The group needs to have been together for long enough to have shared significant problems and had the opportunity to work at solving them and see the effects. These ways of solving problems become taken-for-granted and are passed on to new members. As ways of thinking and feeling they are deeper than the manifest behaviours. They are typically tacit or hidden because they have been passed from generation to generation within an organization and organization members don't see them anymore because they are taken for granted.

Therefore, culture is much deeper than open doors, plants and bright colours and mission statements and strategic plans. When you look at initiatives and why they haven't worked or achieved their intended outcomes, the answer is likely to be that the initiatives violate some taken-for-granted assumptions that are embedded in the organizational psyche because they were successful in the past. That is the key to understanding culture. Because something is successful at some point in time it gets passed on as 'the way we do things around here'. Schein sees culture as the sum total of all the taken-for-granted assumptions that a group has learned through its history. Therefore, an organization's culture is deep – it controls organizations more than organizations controlling it. It is broad and it is stable as it sets predictability and normality and hence changing it evokes anxiety and resistance.

While the notion of culture is abstract, its expression is very concrete. There is no right or wrong, better or worse culture. Appropriate or inappropriate culture only makes sense in the context of what a particular organization is trying to do and what assumptions an organization needs to hold to be successful in its environment.

What are the important elements of forming culture in a new organization? Schein declares that the primary mechanisms that embed culture in a new organization are found in the behaviour of the leaders. What do they pay attention to, measure and control regularly? How do they react to critical incidents and organizational crises? What criteria do they use to allocate scarce resources? What behaviours do they role model? If organizational leaders are the primary sources of culture, then efforts to develop leadership skills are an essential strategy in cultural change. But leadership behaviour is not enough by itself; it needs to be supported by other organizational mechanisms. Some secondary mechanisms that embed culture are the structure of the organization, the systems and procedures, the rituals, the design of physical space, the stories and legends that are told about people and events and, probably least, the statements of organizational philosophy and mission. Take teamwork for example. An organization may espouse teamwork; that is, it says it wants people to work together, to share information and be co-responsible and co-accountable. At the same time, performance is measured individually and ultimately promotion is based on individual work and, perhaps, individual work that is achieved at the expense of others. Hence the message goes around, 'what really matters here is individual work', and so the espoused focus on teamwork is actually negated by existing, more powerful structures. To take another example, the organizational values espouse clarity, but the tacit shared assumptions may be that seeking clarity gets you into trouble and that keeping things close to your chest or deliberately vague is what is rewarded. Consequently, efforts to develop clarity get nowhere. In short we don't examine culture in the abstract. We try to see what shared tacit assumptions are operative in a concrete issue.

Take a reflective pause and consider this section on organizational culture in the light of your experience in your organization.

REFLECTIVE PAUSE

Think about the visible artefacts around you and the behaviours you observe:

- Is there anything that puzzles you, particularly if you have worked in other organizations and have points of contrast?
- Ask someone who has been in the organization for some time why they are this way.
- Does the answer satisfy you?

THE DRAMATIC PATTERN OF EXPERIENCE

Life as drama is a commonly used metaphor. You are familiar with Shakespeare's 'All the world's a stage and all men and women merely players' and you use words like 'role', 'character' and 'acting a part' about everyday life quite freely. Through this metaphor

organizing may be viewed as theatre and drama, where there is a combination of the practical and the symbolic, where people have roles and they enact a plot. Drama is about the
concrete tensions and struggles that emerge in human communities and organizations.
There are several inherent tensions in a drama: within characters and between characters;
and there are two dramas: the inner psychological drama and the outer social drama.

The inner psychological drama is about self-identity and the challenges to adapt to the
outer circumstances of the organization and to learn. In the dramatic pattern of experience the self is understood as a social process. In other words, your behaviour is shaped
by social expectations, the behaviour of others and how you understand them. You present
yourself differently to different audiences because of the different roles you are required
to play in different settings. You are like the stage actor playing the role that is required.
Hence much of social life is a matter of consciously and unconsciously shaping your self-
presentations to make them fit whatever situations in which you find yourself. Difficulties
arise when you do not know what role is required of you and when you are not sufficiently
skilled in presenting the desired image which may or may not sit comfortably with you. The
self in any social situation is defined by three components. First, there is the performance
itself through the word, gestures, actions and props that describe behaviour in the given
situation. Second, there is your interpretation of others' responses to your performance
and that interpretation can be in advance, concurrent or reflective afterwards. Third, there
is your inner response to the performance and the feelings you have about the responses
of others. Your actions are *instrumental* (i.e. in the service of some objectives) and *expres-
sive* (a symbolic representation of the kind of person you are striving to be).

The outer social drama is a function of how roles are constructed and played out, such
as between manager and staff. Plots are a way of coordinating roles and characters to one
another in an ongoing dialectic. The dramatic metaphor allows you to conceive behaviour
as emerging from behaviour of actors who consciously select their lines of action.

BEING 'BACKSTAGE'

Erving Goffman adopts a dramatic approach and points to a distinction between the 'front
region', where performance is public for the benefit of clients and customers, and the 'back
region' or backstage, where public access is restricted. In the front region you are onstage
with clients or customers and you are performing for them. You are representing the organization and its official values and are confined to behaving congruently according to these
values. This front region may have physical features as, for instance, in a restaurant or a shop
where you are on the floor serving customers or at a front desk meeting clients. There are
physical props to support your work – layout, forms of furniture, clothes on racks, cash desks
and so on. There are personal expressions of the front region. You may be wearing a uniform
and go through specific routines. You have to keep a polite, pleasant and friendly demeanour, make friendly gestures and enact your role with care and decorum. Others' dress may

indicate social or organizational status and their manner may warn you of how they enact their role. When you are in the presence of others, especially those of higher status, your behaviour needs to communicate signs that portray your desire to present a good front and then your performance needs to confirm that good impression. Critical to the success of your performance is its dramatic realization. In other words, you must make your performance significant by the skilful presentation of self and by fulfilling others' expectations.

Once you go backstage and are physically away from customers and clients you can relax, step out of role, drop the façade you had for the customers, and say what you like about them. There may be physical forms of the separation between the front and back regions, such as being upstairs or in a room at the back. You may be in a room where walls separate you from the public. If, as is often the case, there is a contradiction between what is publicly presented in the front region and what is done and said backstage, then the physical barrier is important. Thin walls may separate you visually from the customers but you may be overheard. Glass panels may block the sound but you may be seen. Backstage settings may be a staffroom, canteen, toilets, kitchens, your home, indeed anywhere away from the customers.

At the same time there are challenges backstage. You cannot relax to the extent that you are indiscreet or damage others' perception of you. Even if you are venting frustration about an interaction with a customer you need to be aware of what behaviour is acceptable with your colleagues and be aware of what impression you are creating about your competence and professionalism. So the jokes you tell and the remarks you make need to be tempered. Similarly with social media. You might think that you are backstage in using social media but you have to be careful about what you post on it.

Goffman's point is that social behaviour is regulated and that you work to maintain the social order. There are rules of interaction based on assumptions about what is appropriate behaviour. If you cannot find others to maintain your dignity and protect you from embarrassment or from losing face then the social order becomes unstable. You have to believe that others won't take undue advantage of you and you have to show by how you behave that you can be trusted.

Now take time for another reflective pause and apply Goffman's notion of front and back stage to your organization.

REFLECTIVE PAUSE

Sketch out the front region of your organization:

- the setting (physical layout, furniture, props)
- the personal front (uniform, gestures, routines, facial expressions)
- the norms of its performance for others (official values)

Sketch out the backstage region of your organization:

- the physical barrier from the front region
- the behaviours that go on there
- the inconsistencies with the front region

What might these tell you about the organization?

CONCLUSIONS

This chapter has introduced the study of organizations from the insider perspective, what may be called the organizational underworld. The underworld is hidden from the view of outsiders and can only be accessed by those who can enter this underworld and be unnoticed and, therefore, experience the normal patterns of relating and behaving in which its members engage. The dramatic metaphor provides a perspective on what goes on in the front- and backstage regions and enables tracing it in terms of characters, roles, plots, actions and performance. These reflect the nature of human identity in everyday life and provide a device for standing back and seeking insight into the constructed nature of play-acting that characterizes behaviour in organizations. The dramatic pattern holds both the practical and the symbolic and uncovers what may be understood under the surface of the lily pond of your organization as basic assumptions of a culture and may reflect patterns of organizational defensive routines. The challenge is to uncover what gestures, symbols and cultural rules are actually being used, and how they are socially constructed by exploring what they mean for whom and how they drive action.

How do you study organizations from inside when, as we have seen, there is so much going on that is covert and symbolic? To develop a methodology for engaging in insider inquiry we move to the next chapter.

2

INQUIRING FROM THE INSIDE

A conversation between a student engaging in insider inquiry and his lecturer:

Student: Management doesn't care.

Lecturer: How do you know that management doesn't care? It could be that your interpretation is wrong or that you have missed or overlooked some evidence. What is it in your experience that has led you through interpreting to the conclusion or judgement that management doesn't care? It could be that management does care but doesn't know how to show it. Or it could be that you are so angry and alienated that you are blind to any caring efforts management might be making.

Student: This is a tough question. I need to go back to my notes and reflections to see how I worked through all that to get to that judgement.

The previous chapter introduced the study of organizations through the lenses of organizations as social constructions whose meanings are played out in dramaturgical form within and between employees as actors, particularly backstage, and which hold collective assumptions that form a culture and reflect theories of action. It invited you to pay attention to the dynamics that go on around you in the organization. In this chapter you are invited to turn inward by attending to how you think about what you observe and experience in your organization. While this may seem to be the opposite of the outward-oriented focus of the organizational dynamics that run through this book, this is not so. Learning how you think is an essential part of approaching the exploration of

organizations from the inside. Judi Marshall refers to inner and outer arcs of attention, by which she means that you be attentive, not only to what is going on around you (the outer arc) but also to how you are thinking and interpreting what is going on (the inner arc). This is not new for you. You have plenty of experiences of attending to both at the same time. Remember an occasion when you watched a film and as you watched it you were aware that you were feeling sad or thrilled by what was going on in the film. Or you'll have had the experience of reading an academic or a technical article and at the same time being aware that you were finding it very difficult to grasp the complexity of the argument or language in the article. In the context of insider inquiry this book invites you to attend to both what is going on around you in the organization and to how you are thinking and feeling as you participate in the organization's processes and ask questions about it. More particularly this chapter introduces and invites you to take a stance of inquiring into your experience. It presents the clinical approach as an approach to insider inquiry and as a general method by which you can engage in insider inquiry and consolidate your learning.

INQUIRY FROM THE INSIDE

Insider inquiry begins and works from direct personal experience. Evered and Louis refer to their method of insider inquiry as 'multisensory holistic immersion' in what Schon calls the 'swampy lowlands' where problems are messy and confusing and incapable of a technical solution. As you listen to what people say, observe what people do and question the outcomes of deliberate and spontaneous action, intended and unintended, you can learn to 'decipher the blooming, buzzing confusion' that goes on around you, as Evered and Louis put it. As 'a blooming, buzzing confusion' the insider approach to questioning what goes on in organizations differs from the external approach because neat sets of formulae and frameworks cannot be applied in a uniform and predictable manner. These formulae and frameworks tend to portray *espoused theory* and not *theory-in-use*. How might you uncover *theory-in-use*? This chapter offers a solution.

Revans' learning formula, $L = P + Q$, is at the heart of the approach to insider inquiry in this book. In this learning formula L stands for learning, P for programmed knowledge (i.e. current knowledge in use, already known, what is in books and what prescribes solutions) and Q for questioning insight (Figure 2.1). For insider inquiry, learning comprises engaging in questioning that comes from your direct experience in juxtaposition with the knowledge and research from the field of organization studies. Questioning is primary. Asking what is going on and what events might mean are the foundation of learning. Questioning insight (Q) involves learning to ask fresh questions, to unfreeze underlying assumptions and to create new connections and mental models.

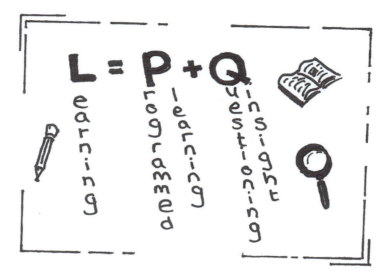

Figure 2.1   The learning formula

TAKING THE CLINICAL PERSPECTIVE

Schein writes about taking what he calls a 'clinical perspective'. His perspective focuses on events that arouse your curiosity. Are there problems and anomalies that are difficult to explain? Here you can look back on incidents and ask critical questions as to how some events or incidents inhibit the organization from functioning effectively. You might, for example, study what happened when management enacted a change, such as changing the roster or introducing new procedures for dealing with customers, especially if these were done without consultation. This clinical approach gives focus to the learning formula $L = P + Q$, as it sharpens the questioning of insider experience and engages that questioning with knowledge of organizational theory and behaviour so as to generate learning. It enables you to build understanding and empirical knowledge through developing concepts that capture the real dynamics of the organization. Here you link your experience and understanding to your reading and to relevant theory that helps you explain what is happening. By adopting the clinical perspective, you can attend to what goes on around you and follow your questions about how your organization functions and so set the foundations for your learning. Experience and inquiry from the perspective of being insiders create the potential of developing advanced management skills that you can draw on in your future career, especially if you become a manager in later life.

Now take a reflective pause and bring the clinical perspective to the organization in which you are working.

REFLECTIVE PAUSE

Reflecting on your organization and drawing on the formula, $L = P + Q$ and the clinical approach, write a reflective note or journal entry out of your answers to the following questions:

- Select what you consider to be a critical incident and map out what happened. Who said what to whom? What happened then? What happened after that? What were the outcomes? What puzzles you? How do you consider this to be a critical incident? How are these events and reactions recurrent?
- Select an action taken by management. What were the outcomes of that action? What did your fellow staff say about it? Were there strong feelings expressed? What does it tell you about the organization?
- What reading or theories help you make sense of what has taken place? How are you linking your experience and understanding to your reading and to relevant theory that helps you explain what is happening.

A GENERAL EMPIRICAL METHOD FOR INSIDER INQUIRY

The starting point for your insider inquiry is attending to the outer and inner arcs. You need to know what is going on if you are to live in the real world. If you want to know what is going on then you need to develop the habit and practice of noticing. As noted earlier the inner arc of attention is as important as the outer arc. It may be true to say that everything that is known began with someone somewhere noticing something.

What differentiates humans from other forms of living organisms is the ability to be self-aware. This self-awareness is central to learning and to learning-in-action because it means that you can be aware of your experience, ask questions about it, come to judgements, make decisions and take action. The structure of human knowing is a three-step process: experience, understanding and judgement, with decision and when your knowing is followed up by taking action (Figure 2.2). You have experiences: you see, you hear, you smell, you taste and you touch. You also think, feel, remember and imagine. You can ask questions about your experience. What was that noise? How am I feeling? You may receive an insight (understanding). That noise was someone dropping a plate. I am exhausted. You can follow that insight up by reflecting and weighing up the evidence to determine whether your insight is correct or not (judgement).

Experience is the empirical level of consciousness and is an interaction of inner and outer events. Not only can you see, hear, smell, taste and touch, imagine, remember,

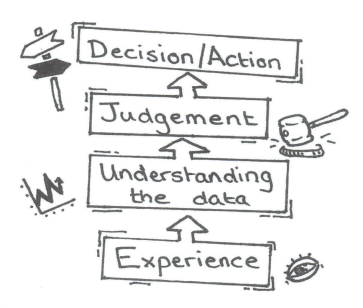

Figure 2.2 The operations of human knowing and doing

feel and think, but you can also experience yourself as seeing, hearing, thinking, feeling, remembering and imagining. Sensory data are what you experience but do not yet understand. Answers to such questions come in the form of insights, which are creative acts of understanding, of grasping and formulating patterns, unities, relationships and explanations in response to questions posed to your experience.

Insights are common; you can get hundreds of them every day. However, they are not always accurate or true. The question then is, does the insight fit the evidence? How do I know that the noise I heard was that of a plate being dropped? This opens up a question for reflection. Is it so? Yes or no? Maybe? I don't know. The shift in attention turns to an inquiry for accuracy, sureness and certainty of understanding. So you move to a new level of the cognitional process, where you marshal and weigh evidence and assess its sufficiency. You can set the judgement up conditionally – if the conditions have been fulfilled, then it must be true or accurate. There may be conflicting judgements and you may have to weigh the evidence and choose between them. Through judgement you can use terms like accurate, correct and true. You also need to distinguish between judgements of fact and judgements of value. A judgement of fact affirms that something is true/not true, or is correct/not correct. A judgement of value affirms that something is good/bad, important/unimportant and may lead to a decision and action.

Human knowing is not any of these operations on their own. All knowing involves experience, understanding and judgement. Of course, you are not always attentive to experience. Understanding may not spontaneously flow from experience. Many insights may be wrong. You may take short cuts and go with the first answer you come up with or the one that is most convenient without testing your answer. Interpretations of data may be superficial, inaccurate, biased; judgements may be flawed. You can gain insight into these negative manifestations of knowing by the same three-fold process of knowing. The pattern of the three operations is invariant in that it applies to all settings of cognitional activity, whether solving a crossword clue, solving an everyday problem or engaging in scientific research. To reject or dismiss this pattern involves experience, understanding and judgement and, paradoxically, confirms it.

How do you know that it is raining? Your sensory experience is to see water falling past the window. Your insight is that it is raining. But that of itself does not tell you that it is raining. Other solutions are possible. It could be that there is a leak overhead or someone is watering window boxes above. So you check for other evidence and you notice that there is water falling some distance away from the window and that people are putting up umbrellas or quickening their walking pace. With this accumulation of evidence you have checked your initial insight and affirmed it and now you can judge with confidence that it is indeed raining. In your insider inquiry you are, in effect, asking three questions: What is occurring? How might that be occurring? Is it so?

Take a reflective pause to begin to catch yourself thinking as you work on a problem. This reflective pause aims to get you started on attending to how you come to know.

REFLECTIVE PAUSE

Take a crossword puzzle, a Sudoku or mind puzzle on your computer:

- What is your experience of the data (the word clue and number of letters in the crossword, the blanks and numerical clues in the Sudoku, the set-up in the mind puzzle)?
- What comes to you as a possible answer?
- Test this answer to see if it fits.

When you have an answer that fits all the evidence (other words crossing the crossword answer, the compatibility of all your numbers in Sudoku, the puzzle solved) note your satisfaction that you know.

THE LADDER OF INFERENCE

The *Ladder of Inference* is a tool that distinguishes between what you know (i.e. insight verified by judgement) and what you infer, attribute, assume or jump to conclusions about and which you hold privately and do not test (Figure 2.3). It works very simply. To take an example. You have been asked to head up a small project group on a particular issue relating to customer service. You invite colleagues you think could contribute to the project and call the group together for its first meeting. Joe turns up ten minutes after the meeting has started. While you see and hear lots of things as the meeting progresses your mind focuses on Joe being late for your meeting. In your mind you interpret Joe's tardiness as meaning that he is not interested in the project, that is your project. You assume that this interpretation is correct and you draw the conclusion that Joe is not interested and cannot be relied on to deliver on the project. So you don't invite him to the next meeting and you exclude him from your project team. Notice what you have done here. Of all the behaviours you have noticed going on at the meeting you have selected the time of Joe's arrival, put your interpretation on it, drawn your own conclusions and acted on the basis of those conclusions. All these activities have taken placed privately in your head and you have tested none of the steps you have taken. In the imagery of the ladder you have climbed up the rungs from what was directly observable (when Joe arrived at the meeting) to a whole theory of your relationship with Joe, all on very flimsy evidence. There may be a number of very acceptable reasons for why Joe arrived ten minutes late for the meeting but you didn't ask. Of course, if you had asked you might

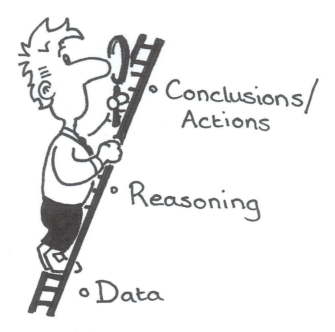

Figure 2.3   The Ladder of Inference

have received a reason that you didn't accept and considered to be a lame excuse, so testing your inferences may be more complex than it might appear. What's subversive about the Ladder of Inference is that you are making inferences as if they were facts. You are assuming that you have all the data you need, that the data you have selected are real data and that your interpretations and decisions are the truth. Notice how you (and others) frequently engage in distorting data when you mind read (deciding what others are thinking and feeling), fortune tell (decide what is going to happen in the future), over-generalize, assume the worse, magnify or minimize the seriousness of an issue and jump to conclusions.

Learning to appropriate your intellectual activities and catch the differences between what you know and what you infer means to become aware of them, be able to identify and to distinguish them, to grasp how they are related and to be able to make the process explicit. Accordingly, you not only experience, understand and judge the world around you (the outer arc of attention) but you experience, understand and judge your own process of knowing and learning (the inner arc of attention). The cognitional operations of experience, understanding and judgement form a general empirical method which requires:

- being attentive to inner and outer arcs of experience
- being intelligent in envisaging possible explanations of those experiences
- being reasonable in preferring as probable or certain the explanations that provide the best account for the experiences.

Appropriating your own knowing process does not happen in one single leap; it is a slow painstaking developmental process that is founded on your attention to the operations of knowing in the unfolding of your own experience. Kahneman, in his international bestselling book *Thinking Fast and Slow*, explores two ways of thinking:

- System 1 operates automatically where there is little or no effort needed to come up with an answer, such as a simple arithmetic question, what is 2 + 2. Kahneman's caption is WYSIATI (**W**hat **Y**ou **S**ee **I**s **A**ll **T**here **I**s).
- System 2 is where we are required to stop and think and we have to exercise self-control in working out an answer. It takes effort.

The clinical approach through $L = P + Q$ challenges the automatic answer and proposes that there is more to what goes on in an organization than what you can see. Throughout his book, Kahneman provides examples of how System 1 can provide the lazy answer, where you can apply causal thinking inappropriately and jump to conclusions. The challenge in insider inquiry is not to jump to accept the lazy answer, the one that 'everyone knows'.

FORMS OF LEARNING

As you engage with learning about your knowing you may get the insight that there are different types of learning. You may notice that some of your learning enables you to continue to think and act in the way you have done before but now more effectively. This form of learning is frequently called *single-loop learning* which is, in effect, learning how to solve routine problems within an existing frame of reference. You may also come to notice that some learning challenges you to think differently by questioning the questions you are currently asking and effectively pushing you to think differently about the situation. This is called *double-loop learning*, and is, in effect, learning how to learn. Single- and double-loop learning are important ways of understanding learning about uncovering theory of action. See in Figure 2.4 that when you have an outcome that was not the one you intended you can take a single-loop approach and try to understand what you did wrong or not as skilfully as you had hoped. When questioning your actions fails to resolve your problem, then you may be challenged to question your initial assumptions or reading of the situation and so change your mindset. This is double-loop learning.

A third form of learning is called *triple-loop learning*, which is, in effect, about developing the practice and skills of double-loop learning. What, then, is the key to spotting the difference? In answer we introduce the notions of reflection and critical thinking.

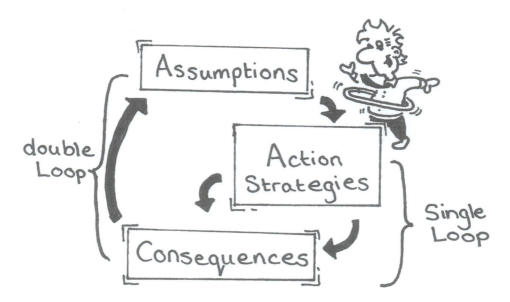

Figure 2.4 Single- and double-loop learning

REFLECTION

Reflection is normally explained as a process of standing back from experience to question it and to have insights. It involves not simply describing experience but doing some analysis through exploring links between behaviour and outcomes, questioning ideas and assumptions, seeking understanding. Reflection can be done after the fact where you can reflect on an incident after it has taken place. This is usually referred to as reflection-after-action or reflection-on-action. The problem about reflection-on-action is that the incident is over and perhaps nothing can be done now. The hoped-for skill is to learn to reflect-in-action, where by being attentive to the inner and outer arcs as events are taking place you can say or do something that shapes the direction of what is taking place.

Reflection is built into the general empirical method. By questioning what happened or what is happening you can seek insight and move to judgement. You can question what others did and said and what you were thinking and feeling and what you said and did. You can question your answers, how you came to these answers and whether these answers fit.

Learning to engage in reflective writing is an important skill. In many professions it is a requirement to engage in continuing professional development. In many programmes and courses students are required to write reflective essays and to keep a learning journal. Appendix 1 provides an introduction to keeping a learning journal and Appendix 2 to writing a reflective essay.

CRITICAL THINKING

There are many definitions of critical thinking. At the heart of all the definitions is that it is a process of questioning, challenging or appraising your own (and others') thinking so as to be able to defend and justify your conclusions. It has three core elements: an act of judgement, evidence for that judgement and the reasoning that led to it. These are integrally linked in that the judgement must be based on evidence of experienced-based facts and you must be able to show the reasoning that led from the evidence to the judgement. That was the challenge for the student in the vignette at the opening of this chapter.

Critical thinking involves a recognition and acknowledgement of your biases. Bias can mean many things. It can refer to values, preferences and interests in everyday life (i.e. anything from chocolate to classical music). It can refer to a group phenomenon that is a structural block to development, such as racism or sexism. It can be a sort of halo effect where, because you are so enamoured with a person or a position, you don't ask critical questions.

The general empirical method provides a method for engaging in critical thinking. It challenges you to be attentive and to pose questions, not only about what is going on around you, but also about how you are framing your interpretations. In other words, the general empirical method works with both inner and outer arcs of attention and does not treat external situations without taking into account the corresponding thinking of the person and does not treat a person's thinking without taking account of the corresponding external situation.

Of course, a lot of what you think you know is actually belief. Belief is where you accept the testimony of others. The critical question, then, is, on what basis do you believe the other? Can you subject this belief to the same critical questioning?

CONCLUSIONS

In this chapter, you have been invited to adopt a learning approach captured by the learning formula $L = P + Q$, to engage in inquiry from the inside or from the 'swampy lowlands'. Insider inquiry begins and works from direct personal experience and requires a method that accommodates that direct experience and closeness, and a framework to work with the 'blooming, buzzing confusion' that characterizes the messiness of daily life in an organization. Returning to Kahneman, while System 1 thinking is fast, there is no substitute for the more extended and detailed processes of critical thinking that insider inquiry demands. When you adopt the clinical perspective, you begin to pay attention to what goes on around you and to what questions are evoked about how the organization functions. The general empirical method of being attentive to experience, being intelligent in your understanding and being reasonable in your judgements sets the foundations for your learning out of $L = P + Q$. By attending to both the inner and outer arcs, you attend not only to what is going on around you but also to what is going on in your own mind. Remember you have little control over your experience. You have some control over your insights and understanding. You have a lot of control over the judgements you make. The next chapter remains focused on you and how you learn, and provides frameworks for reflection on how you engage with others in your work setting.

3

PERSONAL LEARNING IN THE WORKPLACE

In the backstage of a boutique the emphasis on meeting sales targets was reinforced at the weekly staff meeting by two mechanisms. As the sales figures for each staff member were posted on the board the member with the best sales per hour was announced to be 'star of the week' and the three members with the lowest sales figures were posted on a 'wall of shame'. Some members who found themselves on that wall were upset; others laughed it off and appeared to relish the notoriety.

Engaging in the workplace, especially in the context of being on placement or in an internship, provides a rich setting for personal learning. As you interact with superiors, colleagues and customers/clients on organizational tasks you learn, not only how to perform the organizational tasks that your job requires but also how to be a productive colleague and employee. In this book I am placing a central emphasis on developing a spirit of inquiry. A spirit of inquiry is grounded in being attentive to what is going on around you (the outer arc of attention) and within you (the inner arc of attention), noticing the questions that arise and seeking insight to be verified by judgement. Most of the chapters focus on applying the general empirical method to your insider organizational settings. In this chapter the focus is on you and your own learning about yourself through your organizational engagement.

In Chapter 1 I introduced the dramatic pattern of experience that uses the images of life as drama and our actions as roles. I referred to the rules of relationships and interaction, i.e. that every person is sacred and so you must show appropriate deference and maintain face. Interpersonal interactions must be fair. For example, if you destroy others' façades and have them lose face and do not give them their due, you become dangerous to others and they will avoid you. If you claim more in a situation than you can deliver then others feel cheated, feel that they have to invest more than they get and they will avoid you. If you lose face by not having your claims confirmed you lose your self-esteem. If you misunderstand your role in a given situation others cannot play their role and the situation deteriorates. So there are rules of face and ways of dealing with anxiety, embarrassment and emotion. A question for insider inquiry may be to ask if it is the violation of rules of face that explains anxiety, anger, embarrassment, defensive behaviour and so on. I invited you to inquire into the rules of your organizational situation, what roles you have and what lines you are expected to recite.

As explored in Chapter 1, you live in a world mediated by meaning. Meaning is understood as being constructed and maintained through social interaction; therefore, the source of meaning is intrinsically social. Hence, the rules, roles and scripts that hold an organization together are valid objects of inquiry. Through your experience you can sense what these rules and roles are and then inquire into them, receive and test insights.

There is a sense that through your engagement in the organization the self that is you emerges as a result of social interaction. Categories emerge that describe the self – shy, friendly, creative, reliable and so on. Some aspects of the self are public and others are private. You perform in public and also in private. Roles are given to you by others and you can play several roles at once. This emerging self has three components: your performance through your actions and behaviour, how others interpret your performance and respond to it, and your inner feelings in response to both.

In later chapters I will introduce a notion of systemic health in terms of four elements: a sense of identity and purpose, the capacity to adapt to changing external and internal circumstances, the capacity to perceive and test reality, and the internal integration of subsystems. Here, I note that as an individual you may develop a sense of who you are, be able to adapt to different and changing situations in which you find yourself, be able to live in the real world and to integrate your cognition and emotions, your health, work and social life so that you can be judged to be healthy in a constantly changing environment. You are continually taking in information, processing it and adapting behaviour and getting feedback as you move in and out of different situations. Consequently, you can frame life as a cycle of continuous coping and adaptation. This chapter explores ways of framing your personal learning in the workplace, of learning how 'the I watching the me in action'. To this end two constructs that provide frameworks for self-learning are introduced: the JOHARI Window and Transactional Analysis.

THE JOHARI WINDOW

As noted above your engagement in organizations enables you to think about how you learn about yourself. The JOHARI Window (named after its two creators Joe Luft and Harry Ingram) is a four-paned window that captures two variables – what you know about yourself and what others know about you – and plots them against one another in a 2x2.

- Pane 1 - what you know about yourself and others know too is called the OPEN pane.
- Pane 2 - what you don't know about yourself but others do is called the BLIND pane.
- Pane 3 - what you know about yourself but others don't know is the PRIVATE pane.
- Pane 4 - what you don't know about yourself and others don't know either is the UNKNOWN pane. This pane reflects what no one knows, for example unconscious memories or the future.

When you interact with others you may extend the boundaries of your JOHARI window panes. For example, when you tell someone something about yourself that the other didn't know you are extending your OPEN pane and diminishing your PRIVATE pane. When you receive feedback on your behaviour or performance then your BLIND pane is diminishing. As you engage with others in the workplace and on occasions when you socialize with

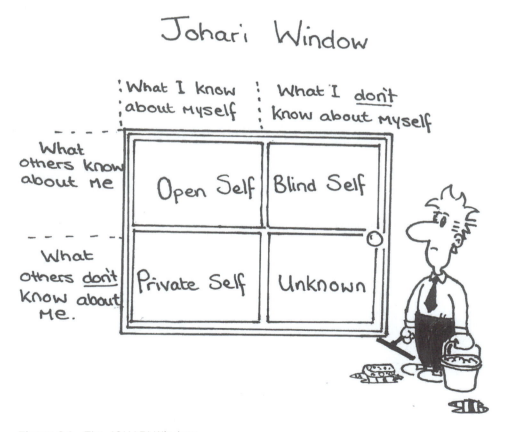

Figure 3.1 The JOHARI Window

your work colleagues people get to know you and part of your life and work which are in the OPEN pane. Your work colleagues see things about you that you don't see (BLIND). You tell some people about yourself (PRIVATE). Accordingly, there is a great deal of personal learning available to you through your participation in the organization. The JOHARI Window can help you ground your experience, i.e. inform what you are doing when you are interacting with others. It can also help you think about what you choose to do. What do you reveal about yourself, to whom? To what do you respond? What roles do you play?

Individuals' JOHARI window panes are not the same size. Individuals who are more introverted and reserved in talking about themselves may have a larger PRIVATE pane than those individuals who wear their heart on their sleeve who'll have a larger OPEN pane. Individuals who are self-unaware may have a larger BLIND pane. The UNKNOWN pane is, by definition, infinitely large.

You participate in the organization as an individual with a formal contract and its accompanying relational process. What have you learned about yourself in how you relate to the organization? What have you learned about how you motivate or alienate yourself in this setting? What expectations have you learned to have (or not have) about being an employee, albeit on a temporary basis? What are you learning about your theory of action?

As you reflect on your participation in your team or work unit what insights into yourself have you received about working with others, especially individuals who are different from you and with whom you find it difficult to relate? Have you learned about the kind of team player you are (or are not)? Have you learned what areas of team participation and skills you need to develop?

In relation to the wider system in which you work, on occasions where you have had to cross familiar team boundaries and engage with other teams or functional areas that do different work, what have you learned about yourself?

Your ongoing interaction with superiors, colleagues and customers/clients contributes to how you are developing the self that will become you and open up elements that are currently in your BLIND pane. You develop a sense of colleagues with whom you work, and how you interact with others may help them learn about themselves (their BLIND pane).

Take a reflective pause to apply the JOHARI Window to yourself in your organization.

REFLECTIVE PAUSE

- Draw your JOHARI Window with respective weightings to the size of the four panes with respect to yourself.
- Reflect on an interaction through which the size of one of your panes increased or decreased.

TRANSACTIONAL ANALYSIS

The Transactional Analysis (TA) literature shows that there are three aspects to your personality, 'ego states': *Parent*, *Adult* and *Child*. These are psychological realities and do not refer to biological parenthood or chronological age. They refer to patterns of thinking, feeling and behaving that you have introverted from your childhood. The *Parent* in you refers to the part of you that is reflected by what you have been taught, ways of thinking, feeling and behaving that you have internalized from parental figures in your past. Just as biological parenthood has two roles, nurturing and critical, so does the psychological *Parent*. Therefore, *Nurturing Parent* is that part of you that nurtures. So when someone is being helpful to you we can say that this is a demonstration of *Nurturing Parent*. Benevolent problem solving, advice giving and expressions of care are signs of *Nurturing Parent*. There is another side of *Parent*, namely *Critical Parent*. This is the part of *Parent* that is controlling and critical. Demonstrations of *Critical Parent* are found in the use of evaluative adjectives like 'good', 'bad' and 'disgraceful'. *Critical Parent* verbs tend to be ones like 'should' and its synonyms, 'ought', 'have to' and, of course, the negative 'shouldn't have'. Favourite *Critical Parent* adverbs are 'always' and 'never', as in 'you should never do that'. Accompanying behavioural manifestations tend to be the pointed or wagging finger, furrowed brow or sterns expression of disapproval.

Figure 3.2 The three ego states

The *Adult* state is a psychological state and does not refer to adult in the usual way we mean it. The *Adult* in you inquires into the factual situation in an unemotional way. When? What? How much? It also processes what is happening in the *Parent* and *Child*. It is mistaken to think that you can be in the *Adult* all the time.

The third state is the *Child*. Again this does not refer to chronological age but to patterns of thinking, feeling and behaving. The *Child* in you is that part of you that is the source of your feelings and creativity and is expressed in different ways. The *Free* (or *Spontaneous*) *Child* is where you feel uninhibited and you go along with how you are feeling. The *Adapted Child* is where you have been socialized into how to get along with other people. The *Little Professor* captures the notion of the manipulative *Child*.

You may find yourself being sucked into your *Parent* and your *Child* in the face of what goes on in your organization. For instance you may catch yourself complaining about the behaviour of a colleague or boss and notice you are having a *Parent* response. 'She shouldn't have done that!' 'He should be more considerate!' If you experience what you consider to be inequitable or unfair treatment or think that you weren't consulted sufficiently, you may catch yourself being in your *Child* and wanting to punish the manager by not cooperating or reducing your work energy in the form of sulky *Child*, 'I'll show him!' The *Adult* may play a role here by noticing how you are getting trapped into your *Child* and perhaps getting yourself into trouble by offering a less emotive perspective for you to consider and the possibility of standing back from the heat of the situation.

As you interact or transact with others you do so with your *Parent*, *Adult* or *Child*. The *Parent*, *Adult* or *Child* in you can address and receive a response from the *Parent*, *Adult* and *Child* in the other. This can work in a simple complementary manner or in a crossed or complex manner. An example of a complementary transaction is when you ask the time (your *Adult* seeking information) and the response is to tell you the time (the *Adult* in the other providing the information requested). If, on the other hand, you (in your *Adult*) ask the time and the response you get is an irritated 'Don't bother me, can't you see I'm busy?' (*Parent* or *Child*) then the transaction has been crossed as the response has come from an ego state other than the one to which the question was addressed. Communication breaks down and a bad taste in left in both parties. Of course, 'What time is it?' can be asked in a context and tone of voice that is really coming from *Critical Parent* (saying, in effect, 'you are late'). If you perceive a comment by your manager as a criticism, you may notice yourself responding from your *Child* – 'It wasn't my fault'. The responses to being posted on the 'wall of shame' described at the top of this chapter evoked *Compliant Child* in those members who felt upset and *Spiteful Child* in those who laughed it off.

Some transactions recur as games. A game is a series of psychological transactions between two people, which appears on the surface to be straightforward and honest, but actually has an ulterior motive that results in a negative outcome. A typical negative outcome is that someone is put down or that we discount ourselves. Games are a way that some people structure their relationships, particularly in the workplace, and make them predictable as a way of confirming a negative approach to life. The names that games are given tend to be self-expressive and portray what the game is about – for example, Mine's

35

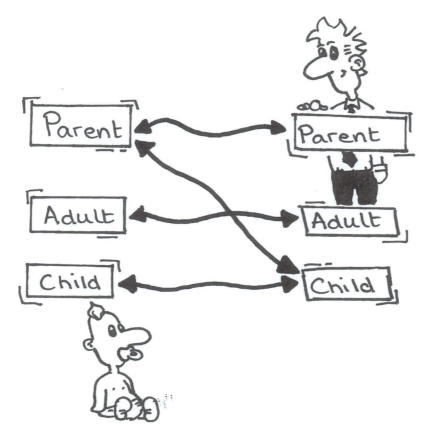

Figure 3.3 Transactional Analysis

Better than Yours, Stupid, Wooden Leg, Blemish, Harried, Rapo, Helpless, Look at What You Made Me Do, Why Don't You ... Yes, But If It Weren't for You, Uproar ...

Games provide an insight into your own behaviour and your own action theory. There are two challenges. One is to recognize and stop playing the games that you might play. Be yourself without needing to discount others or yourself. The other is to recognize the hook in a game that another person is trying to get you to play and not to play the complementary role, thereby stopping the game from developing. You may notice that bullying behaviour tends to express *Critical Parent* and seeks a corresponding *Child* response. If this is you, do you choose to play?

Organizations may also encourage game playing, where *Parent-Child* transactions predominate, and games such as, Harried, Blemish, Gotcha, Poor Me, Don't Ask Me and others are staple food. These reflect systemic, covert or defensive routines that inhibit effectiveness and organizational learning.

The learning challenge when you engage in conversations or transactions is to learn to recognize how you may get sucked into an ego state by others in certain situations. This is not always easy and a more serious application of Transactional Analysis, beyond this superficial introduction, is to learn that responses are deeply rooted in unconscious memories that may require skilled help to uncover. In short, Transactional Analysis provides a tool for you to develop insight into your BLIND pane by catching spontaneous emotional responses that come from buried memories. The general empirical method enables you to recognize the transactions for what they are and not to be seduced into a reactive behaviour that is being driven by the behaviour of the other and that hooks something in you. It enables you to recognize what is going on in you and in the situation, and by identifying and weighing insights to form a judgement, you may choose how to behave. You can decide how you want to behave as a work colleague, a subordinate or a manager. You can choose not to bully others, not to play victim, not be seduced into putting others down and so on. Transactional Analysis gives you a useful framework for catching when that might happen and for changing your reaction and response. Thus you learn to get to know yourself and to take responsibility for who you are and how you behave.

Take a reflective pause to consider your reactions and responses to what is said to you in your organization.

REFLECTIVE PAUSE

Reflect on an interaction or transaction you have had with a colleague that left a bad taste in you:

- What did that colleague say to you?
- In TA terms how did you experience how he/she spoke to you?
- What feeling did it evoke in you? In TA terms how do you categorize that feeling?
- How did you respond? In TA terms how do you categorize that response?
- What happened then?
- What was the aftermath in terms of further interactions later or continuing working relations?
- How might you respond differently in the future, either with the same person or in a similar situation?

PERSONAL VALUES, ETHICS AND BEHAVIOUR

What does your experience of the workplace teach you about your own personal values and how you value? I have explored how the cultural rules of organizations assume that the person is sacred and that the rules of face generally pertain. While there are laws about bullying, sexism and so on there may be a lot more covert transactions going on that do not reach that classification. 'Treat others as you would have them treat you' (a *Parent* injunction) may be a minimalist ethical stance but it works.

In Chapter 2, you learned to use the general empirical method as a tool to help you capture how you know. Now I extend it to take in decision-making and behaviour. When you consider your behaviour, you need to know something of how you engage in deciding that a particular action is worthwhile. You take action on the basis of what you judge to be good, worth doing, the best option available and so on. In terms of the general empirical method you are essentially adding the activities of valuing, choosing, deciding and taking action to the cognitive operations of experiencing, understanding and judging. So to the general empirical method of being attentive, being intelligent, being reasonable, we now add being responsible. When you are confronted with concrete choices of what to do you typically ask what courses of action are open to you and you review options, weigh choices and decide. You may reflect on the possible value judgements as to what the best option might be and you decide to follow through and you take responsibility for consistency between your knowing and your doing. If you genuinely ask yourself what will you do, then you must ask in a concrete situation as choosing what is good is concrete and you ask what you will do in the here-and-now. You ask in the situation as you understand it. Your simple ethical questions involve you in the effort to understand the situation. That can only happen by paying attention to the data of sense and data of consciousness. The judgement of value is grounded, therefore, in a knowledge of reality and intentional response to value and the thrust to act responsibly. Deciding to act completes the operations of experiencing, understanding and judging as knowledge alone does not change the way you live or make you a better person. Taking appropriate action does.

You do not engage in making value judgements in a vacuum. You have learned values from parents, teachers and others whose insights and judgements of value have been formed by intelligent and responsible persons over generations. Now as an adult you grow to learn your own processes of being attentive, intelligent, reasonable and responsible. You may find yourself in a work setting where values other than or contrary to yours pertain. You may then feel ill at ease or alienated and, consequently, engage in self-questioning about your engagement in the organization and make value judgements about what you might do.

CONCLUSIONS

In this chapter the focus is on you and your own learning about yourself through your front- and backstage organizational engagement. Being mentally healthy and socially adept involves developing a sense of who you are, being able to adapt to different and changing situations in which you find yourself, being able to live in the real world and to integrate your cognition and emotions, your health, work and social life. As nothing stands still you need to be able to cope and to adapt to the forces that change and shape you. Hence how you take in information, process it and adapt your behaviour and get feedback as you move in and out of different situations is a continuous learning process. In Transactional Analysis terms, it means asking what is really going on, checking assumptions about the situation (especially covert) and deciding how to respond in a manner than keeps the integrity of the situation and the relationship and doesn't burn bridges. In JOHARI Window terms, the boundaries between your panes are constantly shifting, sometimes deliberately by you and other times by others.

Some of your learning is likely to be single-loop, where you have learned organizational skills and developed them. Other learning may be double-loop, where you have been challenged to reframe some basic assumptions about yourself by catching how you engage in *Parent*, *Adult* and *Child* states and play games. The general empirical method enables you to learn to appropriate your knowing so that you know when you know and when you are making inferences or attributions. Having that knowledge allows you to take responsibility for yourself, to recognize the areas of choice you have and to have a range of responses by which you can appropriately respond. This is your *triple-loop* learning, i.e. learning your theory of action.

At the core is a spirit of inquiry that is grounded in being attentive to what is going on around you and within you, noticing the questions that arise, seeking insight to be verified by judgement, especially a judgement of value and leading to authentic behaviour, that is behaviour that is grounded in being attentive, intelligent, reasonable and responsible.

Having grounded personal learning in methods of knowing in Chapter 2 and ways of relating in this chapter, the next chapter moves back to a focus on what goes on in the swampy lowlands of the organizational underworld.

4

LEVELS AND INTERLEVEL BEHAVIOUR

Go on a virtual tour of the organization in which you are working. Notice the individuals you see at work, whatever form their works takes. Note what their work entails in terms of expertise or basic training. Recall what you have heard individuals say about their relationship to the organization. Yet, in your virtual tour of your organization you notice that focusing on the individual solely does not provide a complete picture. You also see that the individuals in the organization work with other individuals in groups and teams, and the quality and output of their work together are significant. Continuing your virtual tour across the organization poses further questions as focusing on individuals and teams does not answer all the questions about the organization. You also are aware of teams performing different tasks, perhaps in different locations and how they need to exchange information and to move the partly completed task from one stage to another. Yet this view of organizations comprising individuals who are also members of teams and which exist in an interdepartmental environment within the organization is still not the total picture. You know that the organization exists in an external environment and is constantly concerned about its survival and its profitability in the context of competing with other organizations for customers and clients. You may also note that the organization is part of an industry or a sector, such as retail or financial services or not-for-profit, and that there are challenges that are common across organizations in that sector.

What is being considered in this virtual tour of your organization is the notion of levels of complexity. You are already familiar with the notion of levels of hierarchy, such as position on a chain of command in an organization, such as worker, supervisor, middle manager, senior manager, CEO and so on. But here the focus is on levels of complexity. You have a sense of levels of complexity from biology, whether or not you ever studied it. An order of levels of complexity exists in biological systems: cell, organ, organism, group, organization and society. The order of complexity is that organs are composed of cells, organisms composed of organs and so on. The order of complexity also means that if any of its subsystems ceases to carry out its function, the wider system is affected. Accordingly, a cancerous cell affects the functioning of the organ, which then affects the life of the individual person and has an impact on that person's family and friends. Therefore, a dynamic notion of levels of complexity is needed to more fully understand, appreciate and manage behaviour in a complex organizational system.

The subsystems, which make up an organization as a living system, are: the individual, the face-to-face working team, the interdepartmental group of teams and the organization. The notion of levels also extends beyond the individual organization. An industry sector, such as financial services, retail, health-care, telecommunications, education – where the participating organizations are governed by common regulatory laws, face common challenges and at times may present a common front in order to negotiate with regulatory bodies – may be considered to be a fifth level.

Take a reflective pause to apply the construct of levels to your organization.

REFLECTIVE PAUSE

- What are the levels of complexity in your organization?
- How do you recognize them?
- Can you identify examples of each level, for example different expressions of the individual level, different teams and so on?

LEVEL I – THE INDIVIDUAL IN THE ORGANIZATION

In broad terms participation in the workplace setting is one part of an individual's life. Being employed in a particular organization means different things to different people. For some it is a life-dominating career that is grounded in a professional qualification; for others it is a job with little technical skill and which enables mobility from one organization to another. Employment in an organization is part of an individual's life-tasks, needs and wishes which extend far beyond their participation in any given work setting. Each individual struggles to find unique and personalized satisfactions in this regard. At the same time management's perspective is that individuals fulfil their employment contract and somehow belong to the organization in an appropriate psychological contract.

We know that adults change by virtue of three interlocking cycles: the bio-social cycle, the career-work cycle and the family cycle. The bio-social life cycle marks the stages of development through which the adult passes by virtue of age and their social implications. The career-work cycle marks the stages through which the adult passes by virtue of organizational membership, whether through a long-term relationship, a short-term, part-time or temporary contract. The family cycle marks the stages through which the adult passes regarding relationships outside of the organization, such as family and significant relationships, raising children and so on.

The bio-social cycle captures adults' stages of development from a young adult to mid-life to late adulthood. The developmental psychologists tell us that each stage has its own challenges and that individuals have tasks to face in meeting these challenges. For example, the tasks facing young adults in their twenties are to enter the adult world, to make provisional commitments and to develop a sense of themselves. In their thirties they settle on definite goals and become more realistic. In their forties there is the reassessment of mid-life and the settling into whom they have become. Their fifties are characterized by stability and their sixties onward by retirement and coping with declining energies and health and with preparation for death.

The career-work cycle describes the challenges facing young adults as they enter the world of work and seek to find their place there, through learning to apply the relevant knowledge to do the job and to work with others, particularly bosses. As they progress through their work cycle they may find themselves dealing with being on a short-term contract, making decisions about changing organizations, assessing whether to remain in a specialization or to move into management. In mid-career, they are faced with assessing their ambitions as to what is realistic in terms of achievement and achieving a work-life balance and with remaining relevant to the organization in the face of competition from younger and more technologically competent colleagues. In their sixties there is occupational retirement and the task of adjusting to a new lifestyle.

The family cycle describes the challenges facing young adults as they move from their family of upbringing and negotiate a life for themselves, probably with a partner, becoming a parent and so on. As they move through middle adulthood they develop a new relationship with their ageing parents and in old age may become grandparents themselves.

These are broad themes in the development of adult life and are presented simplistically. While there are patterns in the development of adults, individuals pass through these stages in their own way and in the concrete circumstances of their own lives. Any stage may be disrupted by illness, the break-up of a relationship, death or the loss of a job. Clearly, gender plays a role. The life-cycle perspective emphasizes that in some respects each person is unique and in others they fit patterns of common experience with other people.

What the insights from developmental psychology are presenting is that age matters as the three cycles come together in the life of any individual. How those cycles are balanced and how that balance changes are challenges to the individuals themselves and to organizations. For example, young adults at the start of their career may be willing to work long hours and travel a lot to establish their career. At a later stage they may not be willing to give so much time to their organization and may wish to give the family cycle more priority and seek to negotiate to take parental leave or work flexi-time in order to spend more time with young children or elderly parents. When those children have grown up they may seek to change their working relationship to the organization. The implication for management is that everyone is not the same and that individuals are motivated differently by virtue of how the three cycles interact in their lives. The studies done on the so-called Generation Y and Millennials provide valuable insights into generational differences in the workplace. The challenge for an organization's management is to manage differing expectations.

At the same time and in parallel, the organization has its needs and it wants its individual employees to perform their work and to contribute to the success of the organization. The organization's needs change and it needs its employees to work differently so it may require some employees to do different work and perhaps get training for that work. It may downsize and let people go. These affect the individual's relationship to the organization.

Take a reflective pause to think about how the organization in which you work and the individual engage in an appropriate matching.

REFLECTIVE PAUSE

- What are your experiences of how the individual and the organization matches to meet their respective needs?
- What insights are you having when you hear work colleagues complaining about how they are rostered for work and how that is affecting their need to collect children from school or care for an elderly parent, or when you hear colleagues saying that they feel stuck in their roles or careers or when someone is excited about a promotion or a move to a new unit?
- How well do you think the organization enables individuals to work well and to contribute to the organization's endeavour?

LEVEL II – THE FACE-TO-FACE TEAM

Teamworking, as contrasted with other forms of groupworking, is about task interdependence. Task interdependence is created by the work that has to be done and, accordingly, different types of work and organizational settings demand forms of teamwork that are appropriate and relevant to that setting. For example, teamworking may mean different things in different organizational settings. This insight is critical to reflecting on teamworking in your organizational setting and to critiquing inappropriate models of teamworking that do not fit.

As an individual in your organization you are a member of a team or unit. As an intern you are likely to be joining an already established team. This is very difficult as you don't know the other members and may only be becoming familiar with the tasks to be done. Accordingly you are likely to find yourself somewhat self-preoccupied and wondering how you may be yourself in this team, if you will be able to influence the other members, if the team's goals will include yours and if you will be accepted and liked by the team. These are normal issues to have in a new team and you are likely to find yourself feeling anxious and tense. How you cope with this is important. You may do so by showing how you can be helpful in the team, and by forming friendships. Or you may be inwardly withdrawn and wait for team members to take the initiative to solve your identity and anxiety dilemmas. As you work through these issues they abate and you can participate in the team freely and productively without being so-self preoccupied. If you do not resolve them you remain self-oriented and don't become a productive member.

Teams essentially involve four activities:

1   Setting goals and priorities
2   Analysing and allocating work
3   Examining the team's process
4   Developing the interpersonal relationships among team members.

To be an effective team, members need to have an agreed and shared definition of what the team's mission is, from which goal priorities are clear. The assumption that 'we all agree' may need to be tested and goal conflicts resolved. The allocation of work, job and role responsibilities needs to be clarified so that there aren't ambiguities of expectations and consequent conflicts about who is responsible for what. Process or procedural issues focus on how the team works as a team, for example: what kinds of meetings it holds, what form of leadership is appropriate and how conflicts are managed. Interpersonal issues may revolve around individual differences between people on the basis of gender, race and personality style so that mutual respect, trust and collaboration may be built and maintained between people who are different from one another

These four functions operate in order of importance. If goals and priorities are not clear or agreed then there are likely to be problems with work allocation, process and relationships. If goals are clear and there are problems with allocation then process and interpersonal relationships may suffer. The starting point for any team analysis is its goals and priorities. While the focus here is primarily on the team as a face-to-face working unit, these process issues apply to what is termed 'virtual teams' or teams that utilize information technology as primary communication mechanisms.

Teams form part of a wider system in organizations and some of the dysfunctional issues which arise within the team may originate beyond the team in its technological and political interface with other teams. Problems that arise between teams are considered at Level III.

Take a reflective pause to consider the team in which you work.

REFLECTIVE PAUSE

- What are your experiences of working in your team?
- Are its goals clear? Do you agree on what is important or what has priority? Has this been communicated to you?
- How are roles defined? Do you find that your role is clearly laid out and communicated or are you torn between conflicting demands or ambiguous guidelines?
- How are jobs allocated? Is the allocation system transparent and fair?
- How do you work as a team? How well do you communicate with one another? Do you have team meetings? How are they run? What happens when there is disagreement or conflict? How is leadership exercised?
- How are individual differences and interpersonal relationships managed? Are there opportunities for development in the team, where you can learn new skills and take on further responsibilities?

LEVEL III – THE INTERDEPARTMENTAL GROUP

From the team's point of view, to be effective and enter the organization's life is to work within a larger system, particularly in large organizations where size and distance dissolve immediate personal relationships. This third level is made up of any number of face-to-face working teams such as manufacturing, sales or marketing or regional units whose work must be coordinated so as to accomplish a divisional purpose or organizational purpose. For example, in a restaurant, there may be welcoming staff and waiting staff out front while behind the scenes there are the chefs and those that recycle the dishes and cutlery. For the restaurant to work well, the operations of taking orders, cooking, delivering food and recycling – all done by different teams – need to be coordinated and work in harmony so that customers receive the food that they order, in good time, hot and so on.

The issue at this level is that other units either do different kinds of work and have different specialities and languages or that they work elsewhere in different locations. As you don't have direct experience of working with them, they are sorts of organizational foreigners whose language you do not speak and whose perspective you do not understand or appreciate. Accordingly, the challenge for management is to ensure how coordination takes place and is managed. This is difficult to do as the core of what happens is in-between units, in, for example, the value or supply chain or the flow of information, resource allocation and partially completed work from one unit to another. Discovery of negative information is difficult because it is often hidden in the interfaces that exist between one team and another. This can be a highly political situation where the in-built structures of multiple interest parties may be in conflict. Notice the sometimes aggressive interactions between chefs and waiting staff in a restaurant if food is returned as not being quite was what ordered!

It needs to be noted that small organizations do not have a Level III. A family grocery store does not have a Level III. It operates at a Level II where the staff work as a face-to-face team and everyone multi-tasks – stacking shelves, collecting payment at the till, cleaning the shop – with no specializations. It is when an organization grows and not everything can be worked at Level II direct face-to-face interaction that specializations emerge and structures to manage the complexity need to be created.

Take a reflective pause to consider the interdepartmental group level in your organization, if there is one.

REFLECTIVE PAUSE

From your experience of the team in which you work:

- What is your experience of engaging with other teams?
- What are your insights into how the work flow operates between your team and another one or how other teams are talked about?

LEVEL IV – ORGANIZATION

The fourth level is the organizational goals, policy or strategy level of an organization. It is the final fusion of the three previous levels to form a working, cohesive organization that functions as a complex adaptive system in a discontinuous world. In Chapter 5 you will reflect on the organization through an open systems perspective in terms of five strategic foci – framing the corporate picture, naming corporate words, doing corporate analysis, choosing and implementing corporate actions and evaluating corporate outcomes.

A dynamic within the organizational level is the increasing development of participation in inter-organizational networks, such as strategic alliances, in inter-organizational collaboration and in supply chain management through the extended manufacturing enterprise (EME). If you work in a department that crosses the boundaries to other organizations then your view of your organization needs to take into account how the organization works with its suppliers.

Take a reflective pause to think about your organization as a whole.

REFLECTIVE PAUSE

- What does your organization do?
- Does it have a specialization or a particular niche market or preferred customer?
- Do you have a sense of where it stands in its competitive market?
- What does it do well or not well, as you experience it?
- If your job places you at the boundaries of your organization and other organizations, such as suppliers, how does your organization manage supplier relationships?

SYSTEMS THINKING

Systems thinking is a social construction that provides a framework for seeing wholes rather than individual parts, for seeing patterns of inter-relationships rather than static snapshots. A system is a group of interacting, inter-related and interdependent elements that form a complex whole. It captures how a configuration of parts is connected and joined together by a web of relationships and where we understand how the whole is different from, and greater than, the sum of its parts. A car engine is an example of a system, where each part performs its own individual function but when the parts work together the engine propels the vehicle. Similarly the human body is a system and the body parts are all interconnected and inter-related so that we function. In recent years we have become aware of the systemic interdependencies in the ecosystem.

In the context of your insider inquiry three elements of systems thinking may be useful. The first is that because a system is a social construction you can create your own boundary around what the system is that you want to study. A system's boundaries show you what is inside and outside of the system (Figure 4.1). A system can be a geographical location or an organization (department, unit or function). It can be conceptual or a process like goals, mission, purpose and rules.

The framework of organizational levels is a social construction, that is, it is a framework that helps you develop insights into your experience. You are inside the system and you bring your own constructions of meaning to bear on how you make sense of the dynamics of the system. An important question arises. What is your level of analysis of your organization, particularly with regard to Level IV? Organizations can exist as both at Level III and Level IV simultaneously. If you are working in a branch of a bank, in a store that is part of a chain, in a regional plant of a multinational, in a concession in a department store, which then is your Level IV? Is it the branch or store in which you are working or is it the wider system of which your branch or store is a Level III unit? The answer is that it depends. Selecting the wider system for analysis may be too big for your study. There is likely to be so much beyond your direct experience for you to have access. In a similar vein an organization can exist as both at Level II and Level IV simultaneously,

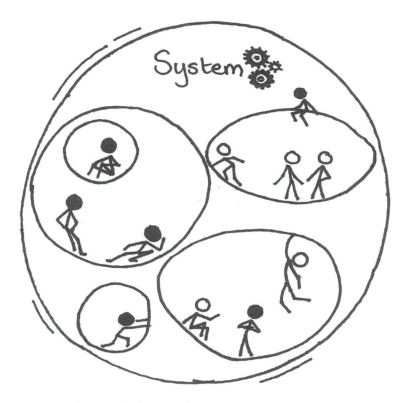

Figure 4.1   People in organizational systems

when it is too small to have a Level III, as instanced in a small entrepreneurial start-up or a small business, such as a family grocery or bar.

The second element of systems that pertains to your insider inquiry is that systems comprise three core processes: inputs, transformation and outputs. For example, a manufacturing company takes in raw materials, capital, people's skills and energy from the environment. These are transformed within the organization into products which are sold or a service delivered. Profits are generated and feed into inputs for the continuation of the organization.

The third element of systems that pertains to your insider inquiry is the notion of recursive systems; that is, how organizations comprise dynamic patterns of feedback loops with many inter-related parts within and across subsystem levels. These loops are recursive; that is, they are non-linear cause–effect relationships, where reinforcing and balancing feedback loops maintain equilibrium. Through its focus on the whole rather than on the individual parts and on the dynamic inter-relationships between the parts, systems thinking challenges simplistic linear cause-and-effect thinking. Linear thinking proposes that A causes B. Systems thinking proposes that the relationship between A and B works both ways, that A is both a cause and an effect of B and vice versa and may have complex relationships with C, D and E. This is what is meant by a system being recursive, that is that the lines (or loops) of cause and effect go in both directions.

THE HEALTHY SYSTEM

The dynamic nature of systems provides the basis for framing a notion of systemic health. Developed from constructs in the field of mental health, the four elements of a healthy system are: a sense of identity and purpose, the capacity to adapt to changing external and internal circumstances, the capacity to perceive and test reality, and the internal integration of subsystems. Taking the individual as a system. individuals need to develop a sense of who they are, be able to adapt to different and changing situations in which they find themselves, be able to live in the real world and to integrate their cognition and emotions, their health, work and social life so that they can be judged to be healthy. Of course because people live in a dynamic environment, nothing stands still. They, therefore, have to be able both to cope and to adapt to the forces that change them and to those forces they shape. Hence they are continually taking in information, processing it and adapting behaviour and getting feedback as they move in and out of different situations.

Organizations as large systems do likewise, albeit in a more complex manner. Consequently, systemic organizational health can be framed as a cycle of continuous coping and adaptation as information is received into an organization, processed and transformed into outputs. This notion of adaptive coping will be taken up in Chapters 6 and 7.

INTERLEVEL DYNAMICS

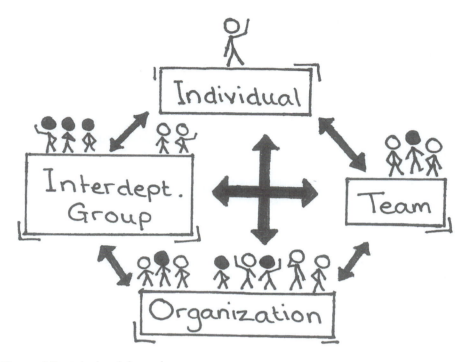

Figure 4.2 Interlevel dynamics

The above description of the four levels of organizational behaviour provides one part of the picture. The additional part, discussed in this section, is that each level is systemically linked to each of the others in a recursive system (Figure 4.2). For instance, an individual's relationships within a team is both affected and caused by how the team works. The work of one team affects the work of other teams. A recession or market change affects all levels. In terms of the systems theory the key insight in a systems approach is to see inter-relationships occurring in mutual feedback loops rather than seeing linear cause-and-effect chains.

The point is that the individual is affected by his/her relationship to the team, by how the team works in the interdepartmental group and by how the organization functions in its external environment. The face-to-face team is affected by how the individual functions in his/her relationship to the organization and vice versa, how the interdepartmental group functions, and how the organization succeeds in its mission. The interdepartmental group is affected by how the organization relates to its environment, how its constituent teams function, and how the individuals and the organization match their respective needs. Accordingly, understanding organizational levels as forming a dynamic and recursive interlevel system increases your insights into what is going on around you.

Take a reflective pause to map the interlevel dynamics of your organizational system.

REFLECTIVE PAUSE

- In your organization what evidence do you see of interlevel dynamics – of one level having an impact on another? Which level on which level?
- What insights do you have of how the recursive feedback loops from one level to another work? How might you verify these insights?

CONCLUSIONS

In this chapter organizational participation has been explored through the notion of the four levels of behaviour. The organizational processes that take place at each level have been outlined. Systemic thinking enables an understanding of how organizations are dynamic entities where there are reinforcing and balancing loops of mutual cause and effect. This construct of the systemic inter-relationship between the four organizational levels is essential for understanding the dynamic inter-relationship between individuals, teams, aggregations of teams and an organization's strategic endeavours in a complex world of discontinuous change. They also lay the foundation of the notion of systemic health.

5

EXPERIENCING THE ORGANIZATIONAL UNDERWORLD

Leslie reported that one day a member of staff whom the newly appointed assistant manager had only met joked with her about some grey hairs she had. She asked him to stop but he continued to the mirth of the listening staff and to her embarrassment. She was later overheard to say that he would regret what he had done when he read the next week's roster. When the roster was published several days later his working hours had been cut considerably.

The organizational underworld is the organization's dynamic life below the waterline in the lily pond image, the back region in Goffman's work or what is sometimes called 'the workplace within'. As presented earlier, the formal frontstage life is marked by rationality while the back region is marked by culture, meanings, attitudes, experiences, feelings, relationships, rumour/gossip, power, politics, etc. It is this covert life that makes organizations different from one another, and interesting and exciting to work in and to study. As organizations frame themselves in terms of mission, strategy and markets, they are also centres of a theory of action, hidden meanings, symbols, assumptions, feelings and covert behaviour. As an insider you have access to the back region and your insider inquiry opens up understanding of what might be going on. In this chapter you are invited to bring your experience to bear on seeking insight into the underworld of your organization. There are very many subjects that could be explored under the heading of the organizational underworld. Several are selected for attention here: the effect of its theory of action, how emotion is handled, the role rumour and gossip play, humour and joking, lying and, finally, demotivation and its outcomes in defensive behaviour. There may be other subjects that you choose to pursue yourself.

THEORY OF ACTION

In Chapter 1 the notion of a theory of action was introduced. What a theory of action emphasizes is how organizations have a *theory-in-use*; that is, the theory that is actually employed, usually tacitly, and is unrecognized by the people employing it. Argyris found that most organizational *theory-in-use* is grounded in an implicit disposition to controlling, winning and to avoiding embarrassment. The assumptions are: be in unilateral control, win and do not lose, suppress negative feelings and behave rationally. The action strategies that follow such assumptions are aimed to protect and defend the self against embarrassing situations by speaking in inferred and attributed categories thereby engaging in a defensive reasoning mindset to explain actions and to implement future actions. The consequences are routines that promote protectiveness, self-reinforcing behaviour, escalating error and ultimately increased defensiveness and decreased effectiveness. But because these routines are unquestioned the decreased effectiveness may not be noticed. Have you noticed situations backstage where your colleagues discuss a current problematic issue and make comments in the vein of 'of course the boss doesn't want to know'?

As Argyris explains defensive routines are thoughts and actions that are used to protect individuals, teams and organizations from dealing with reality. They are reinforced by organizational members who would prefer if these routines didn't exist but defend them as being necessary and part of being in the 'real world'. The routines are based on untested inferences that organizational members make. Organizational members reach conclusions that they believe they have tested carefully, but they haven't because they have been framed to make them untestable because they are privately held. In terms of what was discussed in Chapter 2 organizational members have climbed the Ladder of Inference. 'The boss doesn't want to know' is such a conclusion that is based on an inference. Accordingly, such routines are not discussable and that they are not discussable is itself not discussable. Organizational learning, which we will explore in Chapter 7, is inhibited because what cannot be discussed is kept hidden and is undiscussable.

In summary, an organizational theory of action produces consequences that people do not intend when they deal with difficult problems. It leads them to hold other people or the system responsible for errors rather than examine their own responsibility. They may exhibit collective *Child* self-protective responses to threats that are exhibited in organizational games. It enables errors to be repeated skilfully and organizational black holes in which information is driven underground are created.

Take a reflective pause and see if you can catch signs of defensive routines in your organization. This is not easy to do but is worth attempting so as to gain insight into the hidden world of your organization.

REFLECTIVE PAUSE

Reflecting on your organization:

- What is undiscussable in your organization?
- What makes it undiscussable?
- Can the fact that it is undiscussable be discussed?
- What is preventing what is undiscussable being discussed?

Standing back from any particular incident, what insights have you about your organization's action theory? Can you verify these insights?

EMOTION IN ORGANIZATIONS

As noted in Chapter 1, while the formal organization assumes that the only emotion that exists in the organization is goodwill based on satisfaction, motivation and energetic commitment towards the organization's goals, experience shows that organizations are arenas of feeling and emotion. This is not surprising. People are people and the affective side of their lives does not get put aside when they come to work. Similarly, relationships have rich affective dynamics and they also are part of work relationships. You like working with some people and not with others. You make friends at work. Some events at work may make you frustrated or angry; others have you enthusiastic. You have disagreements and conflicts which arouse strong emotion. In TA terms your *Parent* and *Child* are evoked and you may have to work hard to stay grounded in your *Adult* and judge when it is appropriate to be in a different ego state.

Organizations have an emotional life and this emotional life is intrinsic to their cultural wellbeing. Emotions can be a source of motivation and demotivation. For example a climate of organizational confidence or anxiety can aid or inhibit collaborative work and output. Emotions are often the first response to change. Reading emotions is a management capability. Mostly it involves being attuned to emotions that are being expressed (explicitly) or repressed and being empathic rather than rushing in to suppress or to rescue. It is easy to be emotional when the emotions are happy ones, such as celebrating a birthday, someone getting married or having a baby but it is much more difficult when we are confronted by the uncomfortable emotions of anger, alienation or grief.

For example, Bento explores how organizations have difficulty in coping with grief. She notes that organizations allow bereaved people a few days to deal with the death of loved ones, according to a sliding scale of love: so many days for a partner, for a child, a parent, a friend. Then after that period, with an awkward pat on the back, the bereaved worker is expected to 'get over it'. Any subsequent expression of grief is deemed inappropriate. Yet people cannot turn expressions of grief on and off. While you may be embarrassed to find a colleague in tears at his/her desk, it is harder when you see the person keeping an impassive demeanour and acting out grief indirectly through moodiness, making mistakes, being late and being unapproachable. A Transactional Analysis perspective could be that a collective *Child* is at work where unpleasant emotions are kept out so that there's a false happiness.

ENVY AND JEALOUSY

While the terms are sometimes used together, envy and jealousy are considered to be distinct emotions. Envy occurs when a person lacks another's perceived superior achievement or possessions and either desires it or wishes the other didn't have it. Jealousy occurs in the context of relationships, occurring when a person fears losing an important relationship to a rival. Envy and jealousy may be benign whereby you may desire the qualities of the other but don't wish that the other didn't have them or lose them. They may be malicious where there is a desire to put the other down. In TA terms envy and jealousy are *Child* responses.

EMOTIONAL LABOUR

Emotional labour is a feature of many contemporary organizations. By emotional labour is meant that the expression of feeling is imposed on particular role functions so as to portray a positive perception, irrespective of the particular feelings that an individual may have at the time. Indeed the expressed feelings may clash with inner feelings. There is a requirement that frontline employees of Disney, McDonald's and airlines portray a happy disposition and display a positive attitude constantly. Debt collectors may be under an obligation to portray a stern if not a nasty disposition. The popular notion of 'good cop, bad cop' is an artificial construction that forces both to play a role that may be other than how they may be actually feeling about the situation at hand.

The notion of emotional labour has particular relevance to front-line service staff who are at the organization-customer interface and who are representing the organization to the public. In Goffman's terms it is frontstage activity. Does it involve surface or deep acting on the part of the employee? Surface acting involves playing a part and simulating emotions that you don't actually feel, particularly by adopting the outer behaviour of facial cues and using specific gestures. Deep acting involves you trying to feel the emotion you think you have to feel (a *Parent* response) as you psych yourself into the role. The positive outcomes are selling more products, dealing with complaints more effectively and generally ensuring that customers return. The dysfunctions are that you may experience a dissonance and feel false and hypocritical in a way that may eventually lead to alienation, low self-esteem, depression and stress (a *Child* response).

Take a reflective pause to review your experience in your organization.

REFLECTIVE PAUSE

Reflecting on your organization:

- What pressure is there on your work colleagues (and yourself) to portray a happy and helpful disposition all the time?
- From your backstage experience do your work colleagues put it on as surface acting or do some try to internalize the emotions they are 'supposed' to portray? What outcomes do you observe for those individuals?
- Does having to play a role in emotional labour evoke your *Child* in you?
- What happens when an individual lets the mask drop and reacts to a customer in a manner that is undesired by the organization? How does management react? Are there consequences for that individual?

Standing back from any particular incident, what insights have you about your organization? Can you verify these insights?

RUMOUR AND GOSSIP

While organizations have formal communication channels, such as memos, briefings, bulletin boards, intranets, newsletters, social media and so on, there are also informal communication channels through which employees pass on information through networks of colleagues and friends. This is typically referred to as the grapevine that spreads information, which may be true or false, factual or speculative. In these instances we are referring to rumour and gossip.

Rumour and gossip are important vehicles for informal communication. What is interesting about rumour and gossip is that they are indirect communication, characterized by something like 'I can't remember who told me but have you heard?' The source of the information is not easily identifiable and you might wonder why this information is being spread around. The commonly accepted understanding of rumour is that it is talk that is unsubstantiated by authority or evidence as to its authenticity or truth. It is often regarded as synonymous with hearsay. Popularly regarded as idle talk or trivial chatter, gossip ordinarily carries with it the presumption of having some basis in fact.

Sometimes rumour is distinguished from gossip and other times they are indistinguishable. The basis of rumour is information that is unsubstantiated; it is more public and widely disseminated. Gossip typically occurs in a context of privacy and intimacy and only through and with friends and acquaintances and may or may not be a known fact. It is also conceivable that the initiation of a rumour may be underpinned by some element of 'truth', no matter how obscure or circumstantial the evidence. The extent of the truth or fact is difficult to determine and you may never know if something is a 'white lie' or a 'half truth'. Gossip deals with issues or events of interest to an individual or small group while the parameters of rumour extend beyond a few individuals since its message is of more universal interest.

The purpose or functions served by rumour or gossip are numerous and wide-ranging. Broadly, these are depicted as information, influence and entertainment. The first of these represents an attempt by individuals to better understand their social environment. The second builds on the first by addressing the utilization of information to the individual's benefit. Some contend, for instance, that gossip within organizations may provide a 'survival mechanism' in that it could be one means of humanizing bureaucratic structures. One tangible outcome of this may be related to alleviating excessive levels of employee stress. Finally, rumour or gossip may have entertainment value for its own sake.

Mishra describes different rumour types:

1   *The 'pipe dream' or wish fulfilment*. Such rumours largely express the hopes of
    those who circulate them. One example might be expressing a possible solution
    to a work problem that the employee wants to change.
2   *The 'bogey' or anxiety rumour*. These are primarily driven by fear and,
    consequently, create unease among its recipients. An example of this might be
    a company takeover and the prospect of redundancies in the not-too-distant
    future.
3   *The anticipatory rumour*. These are often precipitated by situations of ambiguity.
    An illustration of this might be whether or not a new general manager will come
    from within the organization or be appointed from elsewhere.

4   *The aggressive rumour*. Here, women may face disadvantage since they are
    more likely to be the subject of sexual gossip. Sometimes, this may stem from
    a perception that female employees are romantically involved with other
    organizational members for the primary purpose of advancing their careers.

A rumour will tend to dissipate if it becomes irrelevant. Once an event has occurred and
the facts have been established, the rumour becomes superfluous. In addition, rumours
may lose interest among their recipients due to boredom, frustration or simply because
they fail to generate sufficient interest.

In your insider experience and in taking up your reflection you may attend to how engaging in rumour and gossip may evoke something of your *Critical Parent* or the *Spiteful Child*,
and so you respond in a complementary mode. 'Wow! That's what I suspected all along about
that person. Tell me more' or 'I'm not surprised given the way she behaves'. 'Did you hear
the one about ...?' You may, in your *Adult*, choose not to get sucked into that complementary transaction and may cross the transaction by inquiring into the truth of the situation.

THE GRAPEVINE

There are informal communication channels in organizations through which employees pass on information through networks of colleagues and friends. This is typically
referred to as the grapevine, the informal mechanism through which rumour and gossip moves through an organization. It demonstrates a healthy expression of the human
need to communicate because it reflects that employees are interested in their work. The
grapevine is unstructured and not under management's control. It moves in all directions –
upwards, downwards, sideways across and between chains of command. It is dynamic
and varied and even fickle. It goes on all day and continues outside of working hours and
works faster than the formal organizational communication channels. It performs a useful task in supplementing the formal communication channels by allowing people to think
and talk about what they fear will happen and how they might react. In this manner, the
grapevine acts as an early warning system. Management may use it to test how a new
idea will be received. A carefully planned leak from the senior management group provides an opportunity for management to test the water on a potentially explosive plan.

Since the grapevine cannot be held responsible for errors and misinformation, and it
cannot be silenced or suppressed, management needs to provide information through
formal systems of communication so as to minimize any damage done by the grapevine.
Rumours can escalate and so management may need to provide hard facts and as complete information as is possible in order to allay fears and reduce anxiety.

Take a reflective pause to study a rumour or gossip that you experienced in your
organization.

REFLECTIVE PAUSE

Reflecting on your organization think of a rumour or gossip that circulated in your organization via the grapevine:

- What was it about?
- What purpose did it serve?
- How did it circulate?
- Did you believe it? If so, how was it that you found it credible? If you didn't believe it, why not?
- Did others believe it? To what effect?

Standing back from any particular incident, what insights have you about your organization? Can you verify these insights?

HUMOUR AND JOKING

In frontstage activity organizations understand themselves as serious places as they work to sell their product or deliver their service. Humour is a backstage activity that lightens an atmosphere, especially if that atmosphere is very restricted. A shared laugh brings people together and enables them to relax. It can help build relationships and trust as work colleagues enjoy being in their *Child*. It can also be divisive as it may demonstrate an inclusion/exclusion divide, a *Spiteful Child* mode. Who is in on the joke? Who isn't? Does the joke reflect the covert humour and power of an in-group? If jokes are told about other people (i.e. the manager), while they may be funny do they leave the question, are jokes told about me behind my back? If the jokes are based on stereotypes (whether sexist, racist or other groupings) they create a wariness and an inhibition that counters the intended light and collegial atmosphere. If practical jokes are played on people (it tends to be only some people) they may create annoyance and destroy trust.

Sex is a frequent undercurrent of jokes. While in the frontstage or the formal organization sexual stereotyping and explicit reference to gender-related issues is regulated, it is common in a subtle form backstage. Jokes are one such form. Across genders, comments about who fancies whom or where comments are made about appearance, sexual innuendo or stereotyping may be quite destructive. What may appear to some as light teasing may be experienced by others as sexual harassment. Sometimes such teasing goes on for too long or there is little sensitivity as to how an individual is taking it. Within gender groupings, the 'lads' or the 'girls', the conversations about the other gender may be quite unsettling and leave a bad taste, but there may be peer pressure to join in and go along with them.

Take a reflective pause to consider on how humour and joking take place in your organization

REFLECTIVE PAUSE

Reflecting on your organization:

- What jokes were told in your hearing recently? What were they about? Were they about the organization and people in it?
- Did you find them funny? Did others? Even though they may have laughed have you a question about how they were received? What is your evidence?
- Are there recurrent jokes that you or others find distasteful? Is the joke teller ever confronted?

Standing back from any particular incident, what insights have you about your organization? Is humour a characteristic of the backstage of your organization? What role does it play in building and maintaining working relationships? Can you verify these insights?

TELLING LIES

Edgar Schein in a provocative article on learning when and how to lie poses a dilemma. On the one hand, as we saw in Chapter 1, the dramatic pattern of experience is grounded in the creation and enactment of social roles where the rules of interaction to preserve the social order require a certain amount of constructive lying where you apply good manners and tact to maintain relationships. Telling the literal truth in many social situations may be very destructive and may destroy necessary working relationships. On the other hand, where management places emphasis on openness, information sharing and organizational learning, lying about results, falsifying financial figures or suppressing unwelcome information are understood as being destructive and, of course, may be illegal. Schein's answer to the dilemma is to posit that lying is not a moral issue in itself. What makes it a moral issue is the intent to be destructive and the degree of harm intended. In Chapter 3 you reflected on how you make value judgements. In the context of this chapter on the organizational underworld, you are being invited to attend to learning how to make a subtle and sophisticated distinction between lying for reasons of good manners or tact, and telling a version of the truth to enhance yourself or put a favourable spin on some event in which you were involved. Do you lie out of your *Adult* or your *Child*?

Take a reflective pause to reflect on the role telling lies plays in the organization in which you are working.

REFLECTIVE PAUSE

Reflecting on your organization:

● What lies do you know are told in your organization? How would you categorize them on a scale from harmless to destructive/illegal?
● What pressure have you experienced to tell a lie? From whom, management or your peers? What did you do?

Standing back from any particular incident, what insights have you about your organization? Can you verify these insights?

THE PROCESS OF DEMOTIVATION

It can be safely assumed that people generally come to a job already motivated and that they are set on the road to demotivation by thoughtlessness and neglect, particularly by management behaviour. Demotivation is where an individual adopts a *Child* stance and, over time, becomes angry at how he/she has been treated, makes various unsuccessful attempts to be seen to work harder and subsequently adopts a disillusioned position. At that point he/she either leaves the organization or adopts a sulky *Child* stance of working the system and grumbling persistently. Leaving the organization may not be a viable option, particularly in an economic recession, so the disillusioned employee may opt to work the system, which is to stay in the organization and exploit it as best as possible for their own self-interest – securing all the benefits available, avoiding all volunteering and extra work and managing to spend as little time as possible doing anything significant. Persistent grumbling is where the individual always complains and grumbles about conditions and how things are in the organization. Some individuals manage to find a niche for themselves in which they create their own private enclave and reduce interdependence with others. Ashforth and Lee describe defensive behaviour as avoiding action by over-conforming, passing the buck, playing dumb, depersonalizing and stalling and avoiding blame by playing safe, justifying and scapegoating. The final option is to collaborate with others who feel the same as they do in creating a collective delusion, which in Merry and Brown's view becomes a neurotic mechanism. So there is blaming, hostility, aggression, anger, feelings of frustration and dysfunctional organizational behaviour that bind people into a collective delusion and serve to relieve the organization of responsibility for confronting and dealing with its problems.

Take a reflective pause to think about whether there is evidence of demotivated employees in your organization. Remember that you cannot get inside the head of another person to judge their motivations. You can make judgements about how your organization works.

REFLECTIVE PAUSE

Reflecting on your organization:

- Do you see evidence of what you understand to be demotivated colleagues who have created their own private enclave of constant grumbling, blaming and complaining? Have they been written off by management and other colleagues?
- Do you observe other colleagues at earlier stages of demotivation? What is your evidence? Are they being noticed? Are the causes being addressed?

Standing back from any particular incident, what insights have you about your organization? Can you verify these insights?

CONCLUSIONS

This chapter has explored some aspects of the organizational underworld, that is what goes on covertly backstage. As an insider you have access to the back region and your insider inquiry opens up understanding of what might be going on. The number of topics that could be covered under this heading is extensive. The handful of topics selected in this chapter is intended to be illustrative rather than comprehensive. The hope is that you will find your own topics, ones that have occurred in your direct experience, that you will pursue them and that you will seek insight into the underworld of your organization. They also provide the opportunity for you to develop insights into your PRIVATE and BLIND panes in how you choose to engage in this underworld.

6

EXPERIENCING STRATEGIC PROCESSES

Jane reported that in the boutique in which she worked the stated mission focused on the customer experience. In this stated mission, staff were to ensure customers felt respected and trusted and that they have a memorable experience in the shop. Yet the practice was that if staff spent too much time with a customer, especially if not effecting a sale, they were rebuked by the manager. Jane concluded that the actual driving force was sales rather than customer service especially when many customers complained that they felt hassled when they entered the shop and actually told staff to leave them alone while they browsed.

In Chapter 4 the four elements of a healthy system were introduced. These are: a sense of identity and purpose, the capacity to adapt to changing external and internal circumstances, the capacity to perceive and test reality, and the internal integration of subsystems. Because organizations exist in a dynamic environment where nothing stands still, systemic organizational health is a cycle of continuous coping and adaptation as information is received into an organization, processed and transformed into outputs. Strategic processes involve acquiring, interpreting and applying information. Textbooks provide frameworks for an espoused enactment of strategic processes. As an insider your inquiry is to learn to be alert to the theory-in-use or *strategy-in-use* in your organization. As introduced earlier, the core challenge is to uncover your

organization's theory of action, especially any mismatch between espoused intentions and what actually drives behaviour. The vignette at the top of this chapter points to a mismatch between espoused strategy and strategy-in-use. The clinical perspective of insider inquiry invites you to be attentive to the strategic processes as they are actually enacted in your organization, be intelligent in how you understand them and reasonable in how you judge them.

Chapter 4 described how an organization is a complex system made up of several levels of subsystems. Now you are invited to consider how these subsystems have a synchronized integration towards a defined goal. This is the area of strategy. Broadly envisioned, strategy is akin to the soul of the organization. In bringing the clinical approach to strategy thinking and action in your organization the questions in this chapter for you as an insider may be how your experience of your organization provides insights, then verified by judgement, to the soul of your organization. How may you capture the elements of its strategy, whether explicit or implicit? In the strategy process interlevel dynamics abound and are important processes to enable you to develop insights into and to learn about your organization's strategic posture and actions.

STRATEGIC THINKING

Organizational strategic thinking is about its worldview; that is, how it views the world that affects its ability to understand and implement strategy. A worldview is filled with assumptions about reality. Strategy is the recognition of opportunity and the strengths to plan for seizing it, but it also recognizes and deals with internal weaknesses and external threats to the organization (what is referred to as a SWOT analysis). These opportunities and threats come from external forces – changes in customers' preferences, competitors' actions, technological breakthroughs, government actions such as deregulation, geopolitical shifts, trends in fashions and other global occurrences. They also come from internal forces – inefficiencies, cost overruns, technological developments and so on. Opportunities also arise from an organization leader's convictions. Mintzberg argues that strategy is captured in terms of five *P*s: *perspective* (an organization's worldview), *ploy* (the manner in which it may hope to gain advantage), *position* (where it locates itself in its environment and what its values are), *pattern* (consistency of behaviour) and *plan* (consciously intended courses of action). These may provide a path of inquiry that may open insights into the more philosophical dimensions of strategy.

Take a reflective pause and consider your organization's strategy in terms of Mintzberg's 5 *P*s.

REFLECTIVE PAUSE

- Try mapping your organization's perspective, ploy, position, pattern and plan as you think you know it from your insider experience.
- Test your insights against other possible explanations.

At the same time you may note that there are different frames for reflecting on strategy. Bolman and Deal's four frameworks – structural, human resource, political and symbolic – provide a challenge to the more mechanistic approaches to thinking about strategy. In Chapter 5 the notion of theories of action pointed to how organizations may act out of mindsets that form a system of self-protection that create defensive routines, which are actions aimed at reducing threat and preventing embarrassment.

INTRODUCTION TO STRATEGY AND THE USE OF THE FIVE STRATEGIC FOCI

Coghlan, Rashford and Neiva de Figueiredo have broken down strategic thinking and act-ing into five components which they call *strategic foci*. They draw on the term *focus* from photography where it means to bring an image into clarity. A photographer accomplishes this by adjusting the lens to obtain the greatest clarity in that part of the image which is the centre of interest. The use of focus is a technique that draws the viewer to the key points of interest in the subject of the photograph as determined by the photographer. In strategic thinking and acting a *focus* occurs when a portion of the whole is clarified in order to attend to it while keeping the other elements of the whole in perspective. The map of the whole inter-related strategic elements is a nonlinear system comparable to a large and detailed photograph of a complex subject. A *focus* is a clarified segment or part that can be attended to in perspective of the whole. The purpose of the five strategic foci is to define the space in the formulation of and actualization of strategic plans in a complex world by complex organizations. Using the term *foci* enables them to be under-stood as five ongoing systematic elements of interaction rather than steps in a process.

The complex process of generating strategic thinking and acting evolves through the following five foci:

1   Framing the corporate picture
2   Naming the corporate words

3   Doing the corporate analysis
4   Choosing and implementing corporate actions
5   Evaluating corporate outcomes.

The framework of the five strategic foci is acting as P in the application of the learning formula, $L = P + Q$. It is through the questioning (Q) from your insider experience of the enactment of the strategic foci that your learning (L) emerges.

FRAMING THE CORPORATE PICTURE

The first focus, *framing the corporate picture*, refers to the basic identity of an organization, answering the question, 'What business are we in or what service do we provide?' An organization's espoused identity is summarized in the organization's mission statement. The mission statement is a fixed set of expressions, which attempts to convey an organization's spirit, task and vision in a brief and concise way. It is fixed in that it represents the best expression in the present time. The underlying assumptions about the identity of the organization as developed in its tradition are critical and powerful forces. These traditions are built on the personalities and successes of the past. Sometimes they are so embedded in the organization that they cannot be seen until some process brings them to light. This is very true in large organizations and in those with high turnover. Sometimes the corporate picture includes the way these traditions govern how the organization operates or whom the organization perceives to be the valued customers.

Take a reflective pause to consider what you know of your organization's corporate picture.

REFLECTIVE PAUSE

Adopting the clinical approach in terms of $L = P + Q$, question your insider experience of the enactment of framing the corporate picture:

- In what business is your organization?
- What is its stated corporate picture? Do you know what it is? Do your work colleagues?
- How real is the stated mission? Is it an espoused mission?
- What is the organization's mission-in-use? How do you know?

NAMING THE CORPORATE WORDS

The second focus, *naming the corporate words*, refers to the determination of corporate words, i.e. explicitly stating the characteristics that allow the organization to succeed in a complex ever-changing environment. These are the driving forces, the core capabilities and the core competencies that result in sustained competitive advantage. Corporate words in this context are different from the 'words' used in the mission statement. The mission statement, while it uses words, is a fixed set of expressions that attempts to contain the spirit or mission of an organization in a brief, concise way. The concept of corporate words comprising this second focus has a more dynamic nature. It is the tactical application of the mission statement. Corporate words represent the forces and drivers that interpret and actualize the mission statement, i.e. the elements that permit the corporate picture to become reality. Naming the corporate words highlights those operations or functions that are the lead operations or functions over time. These driving forces give a unique and special aspect to an organization, separating it from its competitors. These driving forces are central to the articulation, or lived out mission statement of the organization. Naming the corporate words is a look inside the organization to identify, understand and explicitly articulate the main characteristics that allow it to succeed, and without which it would lose its soul. It bridges the *framing the corporate picture* focus with the strategic analyses described in this paragraph to identify the key factors of corporate success.

The articulation of the organization's corporate words goes to the heart of asking the question about what ultimately drives the organization. Is it engineering? Is it sales? Is it marketing? Is it the organization's distribution system? It is not always easy to sort out the corporate words and more than one driving force can propel an organization towards its mission. The identification of a driving force is intimately linked to Level III, i.e. to the functional or departmental level within the organization because a driving force is inextricably linked to execution.

Take a reflective pause to consider what you know of your organization's corporate words.

REFLECTIVE PAUSE

From your insider experience, understanding and judgement, you may inquire into your organization's stated corporate words:

- Do you know what your organization's stated driving forces are?
- Do your work colleagues?
- Are there power struggles across the interdepartmental group as to which function is a driving force?
- Is such power discussable?

DOING THE CORPORATE ANALYSIS

The third focus *doing corporate analysis* involves the generation of actionable alternatives and possible scenarios, and therefore provides direction. In terms of the characteristics of the healthy organization this focus is on taking in information and making sense of it. Sometimes this analysis phase is said to be more important than others. Several streams of academic thought, including the resource-based view of the firm and the industry-based view of the firm lay the foundations for the study of this activity. However, in the context of your insider inquiry you are not engaging in this area of inquiry but rather are attending to how, in your experience, your organization engages in analysis and to what effect.

The methods chosen to do the analysis help determine the structure of the answers and therefore affect outcomes. The task of doing analysis involves the complex involvement of senior management and organizational members in technical analytic activities that also may become highly political. You may have direct experience of specific methods, such as assessment of meeting sales targets (individually and collectively), customer footfall, a daily and weekly sales audit. Bringing the clinical approach to your attentiveness you may have questions about the undiscussable political manoeuvrings and manipulations that occur to massage sales figures and to protect individuals. Here the interlevel tensions between individual and team and between teams may manifest itself.

Take a reflective pause to consider what you know of how your organization engages in doing analysis.

REFLECTIVE PAUSE

- How does your organization take in information and analyse it?
- What undiscussable political manoeuvrings and manipulations occur to massage results and to protect individuals and teams?

CHOOSING AND IMPLEMENTING CORPORATE ACTIONS

The fourth focus, *choosing and implementing corporate actions*, refers to the selection and structured implementation of a strategic plan of action with its dependent components. The process aspect, of choosing and implementing corporate actions, refers to the bias and influence on the selection process that comes from sources other than the analysis focus. This focus is also a characteristic of a healthy organization.

As an insider on placement you are not likely to have access to corporate decision making and implementation criteria but you have access to the actions that are mandated and implemented. You have insider experience of how these choices and actions are implemented and what the conversations are about them, such as if your colleagues are complaining about new procedures being introduced and effectively ignore them. Such events provide a solid basis for clinical inquiry into this focus of your organization's strategic processes.

Take a reflective pause to consider what you know of your organization's direction.

REFLECTIVE PAUSE

- What direction has been chosen by your organization and how is it implemented?
- What are the backstage conversations about what is being implemented?

EVALUATING CORPORATE OUTCOMES

The fifth focus, *evaluating corporate outcomes*, refers to the acceptance of the choice of criteria in the appropriate review and evaluation of the resulting state of the organization. The process aspect of evaluating corporate outcomes looks at the appropriate and fair evaluation of outcomes. This refers to all possible strategic actions, including changes in the mission statement, new driving forces and new methods of analysis in the formulation of ongoing strategies. Evaluation must be unbiased as some changes can be such that a new organizational identity results, occasionally so radically different that the new would not be recognizable from the old.

As an insider you are likely to have access to some evaluation activities and to senior management's assessment of the outcomes of the evaluation process. As you engage in evaluation process you may notice how the defensive routines become more explicit as individuals and teams seek to protect their turf and deflect blame to other teams. Joe, a student on placement, reported that he was never asked at the end of the day how his customer service had gone during the day but was always asked if he had met his targets and completed his routines.

Take a reflective pause to consider what you know of how your organization does its evaluation.

REFLECTIVE PAUSE

- How do you know how the organization is doing?
- What evaluation processes are used? How is progress set and evaluated?
- Are there routines of turf protection and blaming?

THE INTERLEVEL DYNAMICS OF STRATEGY

The overall strategic process is systemic and dynamic. Each of the five strategic foci entails interlevel dynamics of change as an organization seeks to frame its corporate picture, name its corporate words, do its analysis, choose and implement corporate actions and evaluate outcomes. The first focus, *framing the corporate picture*, deals with the key individuals and the history of the organization as it comes to affect strategy formulation and implementation. The contents of this focus are on the core mission and its statement of the organization as well as the characteristics of the key players. If the corporate picture comes from the senior manager, then he/she works to get the senior management group to accept it and then the interdepartmental group and ultimately the organization – stakeholders, shareholders and customers. A new corporate picture forces the senior management group to set new priorities and allocate work to the divisions and departments in a different way. Interdepartmental issues centre on the new allocation of resources and information flow required in carrying out the new corporate picture.

The second focus, *naming the corporate words*, deals with those operations or functions that had become the lead operations or functions over time. These are most often referred to as driving forces and become the articulation, or lived out mission statement, of the organization. There are interlevel dynamics in choosing the corporate words as functional areas compete for priority and status. For example, those who are not in engineering or marketing, where one or other is defined as the prime function, may feel undervalued and peripheral in terms of their contribution to the organization.

The third focus, *doing corporate analysis*, deals with obtaining critical information and making sense of it. The analytic process acknowledges the appropriate connectedness of this focus to the previous focus of framing the corporate picture and to the subsequent focus of choosing and implementing corporate actions which will, of necessity, follow. There are cultural issues in how an organization engages in analysis. Each functional area has to examine its own analysis and process as well as how the interdepartmental group's function affects others and its output. Each functional area may have its own frames for analysis. It is also a sub-culture, with its own traditions, language and basic assumptions. So each functional level is offering its view of the whole from the perspective of its own subculture in the interdepartmental group activity. How these analyses or 'views' inter-relate or are accepted is critical because when integrating multiple functions, the cross-links between functions are most often the sources of trouble.

The fourth focus, *choosing and implementing corporate actions*, deals with the selection and structured implementation of a strategic plan of action. In choosing and implementing corporate actions, the role of the final decision maker resides with the CEO.

The fifth focus, *evaluating corporate outcomes*, deals with the acceptance of the choice of criteria in the appropriate review and evaluation of the resulting state of the organization. The process aspect of evaluating corporate outcomes looks at the appropriate and fair evaluation of outcomes. The evaluation of the corporate outcomes most often resides with the senior management group and the CEO.

> Mike reflected how the appointment of a new coach in his university sports club led to a change in mission. Hitherto the club operated largely as a social environment for the students to play their sport and enjoy the camaraderie. It was not particularly successful competitively. The new coach focused on competitive success and introduced more rigorous and demanding training schedules and methods. An outcome was that students had to decide whether they were prepared to engage in the new training regimes and compete for places on the senior team. In effect they were challenged to change their engagement with the club and redefine their membership with a club that had a new mission to be competitive.

THE STRATEGIC FOCI AS A SYSTEM

The five foci capture the core processes of any human system, built on five questions (Figure 6.1). Who are we (corporate picture)? What do we want to be good at (corporate words)? How do we assess the external world that affects us (corporate analysis)? How do we make choices and implement them (choosing and implementing corporate actions)? How do we assess how we are doing (evaluating corporate outcomes)? How they are enacted reflects something of the health of the system. Each of the five strategic foci entails interlevel dynamics of change as an organization seeks to frame its corporate picture, name its corporate words, do its analysis, choose and implement corporate actions and evaluate outcomes. But experience tells us that these levels are not only discrete and separate but they are also interdependent and inter-related.

The five strategic foci in strategy formation and implementation are part of a very complex whole. While it is important to understand each focus it is also important to understand the relationships between the foci. For instance there is a close relationship

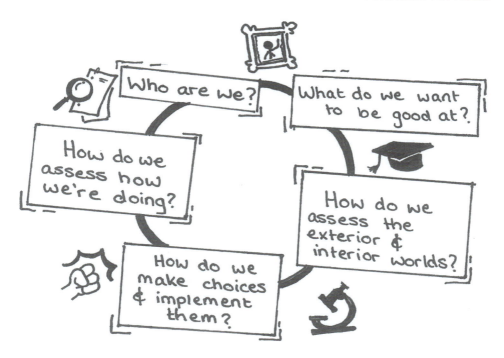

Figure 6.1   The five strategic questions

between corporate picture and corporate words that centres on the implemented skills of the corporate words as an articulation of the core mission. The reverse can also be true if an organization develops a new critical skill. This can force a review and change in the core mission. Corporate analysis may challenge the corporate words as self-preservation may be key to understanding this interaction. The managers in the lead function or driving force may work to protect that status and may be unable to be objective in doing the analysis. Often these distortions are not at all obvious and not detected. The relationships between corporate analysis and corporate decision and implementation are close as forming an open and comprehensive set of alternatives is the basis of making an informed decision. Not looking at enough alternatives or even possibilities reduces the chance of a best decision. The relationship between corporate decision and corporate evaluation needs to be close so that the outcomes measured are the outcomes desired in the decision process.

Your insider inquiry enables you to develop your awareness and understanding of your organization in each of five foci. In this context you may notice that your questions have a different quality about them. When you are questioning outcomes in terms of what was done and how actions were chosen and implemented that produced those outcomes you are engaging in single-loop inquiry. A second or double-loop inquiry can take you from outcomes to action to what was planned. A third or triple-loop inquiry can take you from outcomes, through action, through strategy to ask questions about intention, aspirations and values. In terms of the strategic foci, inquiry begins from corporate outcomes. A first loop inquires into corporate actions and evaluation, a second into corporate analysis and choosing and implementing corporate actions, and a third into corporate words and the corporate picture. In terms of defensive routines, you may have questions about what single-loop and double-loop learning mechanisms are evident and how what is undiscussable inhibits strategic development organization which may not be consistent with its *espoused strategy*.

Take a reflective pause to consider your organization's strategy.

REFLECTIVE PAUSE

- What insight have you now into the systemic strategic processes of your organization?
- Can you verify this insight?

CONCLUSIONS

This chapter has introduced insider reflection on the processes of strategy. Drawing on the five strategic foci as a framework it has posed questions about how your organization's identity, its driving force, how it takes in and analyses information, how it makes decisions and implements action and how it evaluates outcomes are actually done. An underpinning question seeks to uncover the reasoning, both productive and defensive, that guides its strategy-in-use. The answers to these questions reflect the characteristics of your organization's systemic health. Strategic processes reflect how your organization enacts the adaptive coping cycle of acquiring information, taking it into the organization, processing it and transforming it into outputs. The interlevel dynamics capture how the strategic processes affect and are affected by individuals, teams and the interdepartmental group. The next chapter explores how organizations learn and change, and invites you to explore your insider experience of your organization learning and changing.

7

EXPERIENCING ORGANIZATIONAL LEARNING AND CHANGE

The restaurant was suffering losses due to the recession and was in real danger of closure. The owner-manager gathered the staff together and explained the situation. He acknowledged that there was a disparity between espoused and actual policies and that change would need to happen. This would involve having fewer staff and new work systems and innovation and creativity. He received varying degrees of support, toleration and resistance. Serving staff saw their role as fixed with little opportunity for innovation. More autonomy and flexibility were introduced for staff, both in the kitchen and on the restaurant floor. Some staff were fired. As time went on, when the manager asked individuals about how the new system was working, they lied to him, showing enthusiasm for fear they would lose their jobs if they criticized it. In time the new systems began to work. Staff made more suggestions, many of which were adopted and helped to make the restaurant more profitable and to survive.

In the previous chapters you grounded your insider experience of organizations in the framework of organizational levels and interlevels as dynamics systems. Building on the notion of systemic health and having explored strategic processes we now focus on how organizations as interlevel systems may learn and change. The clinical perspective of insider inquiry invites you to be attentive to the processes of organizational learning and change, be intelligent in how you understand them and reasonable in how you judge them.

The adaptive coping cycle of receiving information, processing it and transforming it into outputs is central to learning and change. All learning and change involves acquiring, interpreting and applying information. Hence the emphasis in this chapter is on process, particularly interlevel processes of learning and change.

ORGANIZATIONAL LEARNING

Organizational learning refers to what the total organization (not merely individuals or groups within the organization) can do to increase or maintain the capacity to act in the face of changing internal and external circumstances. There are two basic challenges in organizational learning: exploring new possibilities and exploiting what organizations have learned. *Exploration* refers to the exploration of new possibilities and includes things captured by terms such as: search, variation, risk taking, experimentation, play, flexibility, discovery and innovation. *Exploitation* refers to the exploitation of old certainties and includes such things as: refinement, choice, production, efficiency, selection, implementation and execution.

In Chapter 2 I distinguished three different types of learning *single-* and *double-loop* and *triple-loop* learning. Now I bring those constructs to the organizational setting. For double-loop learning to take place in organizations managers need to learn to question their theories-in-use and basic assumptions, which we introduced in Chapters 1, 2 and 6. As we have been discussing, while organizations have formal goals and strategies that they espouse that govern their behaviour, they often have covert assumptions that actually drive behaviour. These assumptions find expression in the routines of the organization. Some of these routines may actually inhibit double-loop learning. Argyris refers to these as 'defensive routines'. These routines are actions that are implemented in good faith but they aim to prevent people experiencing embarrassment. They are self-reinforcing and become self-proliferating systems of self-protection. They are skilfully implemented and lead to organizational defensive routines which protect them and keep them from being discussed.

INTERLEVEL DYNAMICS OF ORGANIZATIONAL LEARNING

As organizations are dynamic interlevel systems organizational learning involves complex iterations of learning across and between the four levels. The challenge is that people in organizations act collectively, but they learn individually. This creates a tension, if not a frustration, for organizational learning. Organizations learn through individuals who learn; individual learning does not guarantee organizational learning.

How then can we understand how organizational learning relates to individual learning and vice versa? Crossan, White and Lane provide an important framework. They present organizational learning as a dynamic iterative process between the individual, the group and the organizational levels. They integrate three elements in their framework in terms of 4 *I*s (*i*ntuiting, *i*nterpreting, *i*ntegrating and *i*nstitutionalizing) as iterative learning across three levels. *Intuiting* occurs at the individual level and refers to the grasping of patterns, possibilities, similarities and differences and in the work of the experienced professional this becomes tacit knowledge. *Interpreting* also occurs at the individual level and refers to more conscious elements of developing cognitive maps within specific domains or environments. *Integrating* occurs at the group level where shared understanding is worked at through conversation among group members in order to attain coherence. *Institutionalizing* is the process whereby the organization consolidates the learning.

The 4 *I*s hold the tension between exploration and exploitation. The tension between exploration and exploitation is viewed as feed forward and feedback mechanisms. Feed forward (exploration) is characterized by interpreting-integrating and requires a shift from individual learning to team/group learning. Feedback is characterized by institutionalizing works from the organizational to the individual level and may be problematic as institutionalization may inhibit or drive out intuition.

The 4 *I*s have a complementary relationship to the general empirical method. At the individual level, intuiting and interpreting in Crossan, White and Lane's terms are equivalent to experiencing, understanding and judgement. When the individual takes his/her learning to the team level, the team's integrating operations involve the team engaging in conversation and dialogue about its experiencing, understanding and its efforts in order to reach shared judgements. Organizational institutionalizing means that, at the organizational level, experiencing, understanding and shared judgements may lead to organizational action.

These processes do not necessarily move smoothly from one level to another. We do not automatically accept others' views without examining them first. Even more so, groups or teams do not accept the stated learning of other teams without subjecting them to critical assessment. Accordingly, the framework of denying, dodging, doing and sustaining takes account of different reactions and responses to learning and change. The clinical perspective for you the insider is being attentive to movement across the 4 *I*s and questioning how the feed forward or back is working or not working and what it is that is enabling or inhibiting exploration and exploitation.

CHANGE

We now turn to exploring the subject of how people change. What psychological and social processes occur when people seek to move deliberately from one set of ways of thinking and behaving to another? Schein describes how change begins with some sort of disconfirmation; that is, what is expected or hoped for is not confirmed. But disconfirmation of itself is not sufficient for change. The disconfirmation has to be accompanied by a concern about the disconfirmation, such as anxiety or guilt. But that too is insufficient for change to occur. We need to feel psychologically safe to let go of the present and move to a different future. When we are ready to change we can either scan multiple sources of information by reading and conversing with many people to find help. Or we can engage in a relationship with a single source, such as a tutor, therapist or consultant who acts as a facilitator of our learning and change. When we have changed we have to integrate the changed state into our personality, behaviour and significant relationships.

WHEN CHANGE IS MANDATED BY OTHERS

Of course, not all change is self-initiated. Within organizational settings change is normally mandated by others, particularly senior management. What are the dynamics of the change process for those who are being mandated to change by their managers? For individuals, teams and the interdepartmental group, there are three critical process elements: perception of the change, assessment of its impact on the individual and response. The first is *perception*:

- This comprises the *meaning* the change has for those mandated to change, the degree to which they have control over the change and the degree of trust in those promoting the change. How the organizational members perceive what the change might mean is directly dependent on the amount of information provided. When managers say, 'There will be a lot of change around here' and do not elaborate what they have in mind, listeners to that statement are left to make their own inferences and create whatever meanings they wish. Some may infer that their job is under threat and thereby create a negative perception. On the other hand, if managers say, 'There is a continuous bottleneck at the order processing stage which we need to address to speed up our customer delivery service', then the listeners know what is meant and can position themselves in relation to the change which might follow from this problem definition.
- The second element of perception of the change has to do with the *degree of control* the organizational members have over the change. For instance, if the mandated change affects the way subordinates do their job and they have not been consulted and they think that their ability to do their job and deliver a quality service is being damaged by the change, then their perception is likely to be negative. Degrees of control lie along a continuum; at one extreme is no control and at the other full control. Selecting the appropriate position on the continuum varies from situation to situation.

- The third element of perception is the *degree of trust* that organizational members have in those mandating the change. When managers in effect say 'trust us' and everything they have been doing over the past few years has had the opposite effect, why should anyone trust them in this case? Change puts extra pressure on existing relationships. If there is low trust before change, then the change process will not, of itself, increase trust. Trust may be viewed as a continuum, with high trust at one extreme and low trust at the other and varying degrees in between.

In putting these three elements together we can see that if managers do not provide adequate information about the proposed change, do not involve the subordinates and have a low trust relationship with them, then the perception of the change is likely to be negative.

Perception of the change leads to an *assessment of the impact of the change*: any assessment is not simply black or white or good or bad. There is rather a continuum along which assessment is made. The change may be assessed as positively enhancing at one end of the continuum or threatening or destructive at the other. In between are varying degrees of uncertainty and positive and negative assessment. If the perception is negative, then the assessment of the impact is likely to be negative also. Lack of information, lack of control and low trust are likely to lead to a negative assessment. Schein refers to this as 'survival anxiety', meaning that if there is no response to the disconfirming information, then some important elements of the system will fail. Schein makes the point that survival anxiety alone does not suffice for change to take place. A system can be blocked by what Schein calls 'learning anxiety', which is that form of anxiety that promotes defensiveness, resistance and paralysis. A person may experience learning anxiety from the pain of unlearning, from feeling temporarily incompetent, a fear of losing one's identity or losing team membership or a fear of being punished. Increasing such learning anxiety has the effect of increasing paralysis and resistance. It is easy for managers to create disconfirmation; they have the strategic perspective and the hierarchical clout to assert that things are not going well or that change has to happen. They are also well positioned to create anxiety. What they typically tend to be less skilled at is creating psychological safety, which minimizes defensiveness, resistance and survival anxiety.

Perception and assessment lead to *response*. Responses range along a continuum. At one extreme is active and positive embracing of the change; at the other extreme is open opposition. In between are varying degrees of support, acceptance, toleration and resistance that emerge through four psychological stages of change – denying, dodging, doing and sustaining.

- The *denying* stage of the need for change involves disputing the value, relevance or timeliness of the information that frames the need for change.
- The *dodging* stage begins when the accumulated evidence shows that the change is likely to take place. It is acknowledged reluctantly that some change is needed, but that the change is to be dodged; that is, individuals and teams can seek ways to avoid or postpone change or remain peripheral to it.

'Johnson was so resistant to change he never changed desk... Even when his company moved building...'

- The *doing* stage is where the need for change has been acknowledged and owned to the degree that explorations of what changes are required, how, where, at what cost and at what cost to whom are undertaken and the action begins.
- The *sustaining* stage is best defined as the implementation of operating procedures and is a key stage of any change process.

The overall point is that for organizational members to change at the behest of their superiors, the response to change is dependent on a) how the change is perceived (which itself is dependent on the degree of information provided, the amount of local control over the change and the degree of trust in the change initiators) and b) how the impact of the change is assessed. These two elements are influenced heavily by the availability of information about the change and the process of communication between those promoting the change and those affected by it. Absence of information and a lack of a sense of participation create learning anxiety, uncertainty, hesitation and resistance, and increase any lack of trust, which might exist. The clinical questions that you as the insider may ask from your experience of observing how your colleagues are perceiving the change, how they are assessing its impact on them and how they responding are being provoked by the amount and quality of information and consultation.

Take a reflective pause to remember how a change in your organization was communicated and received.

REFLECTIVE PAUSE

Reflect on a change introduced by your manager:

- How much information was given to you and your work colleagues?
- How did you and your colleagues understand what the change was about and what it involved?
- Did you believe/not believe your manager? On what basis?
- Did you have the opportunity and feel safe in questioning, expressing doubts or challenging the change proposal?
- How did you and your colleagues respond: formally to the manager and backstage among yourselves when the manager was not present?
- Did the change happen subsequently and work?

ORGANIZATIONAL CHANGE

Change is a complex process and changing organizations is even more complex. There are three main areas to be considered. The first is the *context* for change. Context refers to a) the external forces in the socio-economic and political environment that drive change, such as capital market demands, competitive forces, developing customer needs and so on, and b) the internal environment such as high costs, budget over-runs, low morale among staff, excessive dysfunctional political inter-group rivalry and so on. For an open system the external forces tend to be the main drivers of change. Accordingly, market knowledge and analysis are paramount. Second, there is the *content* of change – what needs to change. Content of change refer to *what* changes. For organizational systems formal content areas of strategy, policy, technology, organizational structure, work patterns, job design, HR systems and financial systems may be the targets and mechanisms for change. At the informal level attitudes, norms and culture may be the focus for change. The content of change needs to be a direct response to the challenges coming from the context and may make different types of demands on the organization as to what type of change is required. Accordingly, you may also distinguish between different types or orders of change. First-order change describes change within the established frame of reference as in continuous improvement. This is equivalent to single-loop learning. Second-order change describes where change involves creating a new frame of reference, such as how mobile phones have transformed from being merely phones to being computers. It is equivalent to double-loop learning. Third-order change describes developing the habit and skill of second order change and being constantly adaptive to change. This is equivalent to *triple-loop* learning. The categorization of first- and second-order change is also described as adaptive and generative change. Third, there is the *process* of change – how change is introduced and moved through the organization. This is the main focus of this section of this chapter and is elaborated below.

THE PROCESS OF ORGANIZATIONAL CHANGE

Organizational change typically means that individual employees have to change. Individuals may be required to change what they do or how they do it. It may be required of them to change their attitudes towards their work or some particular aspect of it. A consequence of this may be that an individual's matching relationship to the changed or changing organization may be altered, either positively or negatively. An organizational change, if not well managed, may result in individuals feeling alienated, especially if, as we have seen, the change has not been well communicated. A change agenda in an organization typically affects the work of teams. Teams may set new goals and targets; they may have to work differently. At the interdepartmental group level, teams may be merged, resources re-allocated, and technology and advanced information systems may alter access to the flow of information. At this level, teams may be required to communicate differently and more effectively across functions and departments. At the organizational level, the change may result in a new product or service for customers or clients, and may affect market expectations and the organization's image. So we can see that organizational change comprises individual change, team change and interdepartmental group change.

While all change needs to deal with questions of why change, what to change and how, and how to make it survive and work, the interlevel dynamics of organizational change add layers of interaction so that a system may change. Following Beckhard and Harris the following five questions may form the basis of insider inquiry into an organizational change (Figure 7.1).

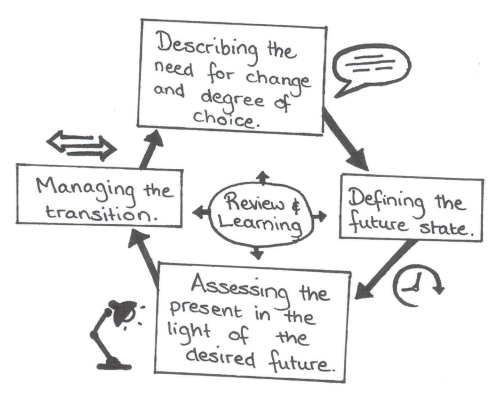

Figure 7.1 The process of organizational change

WHY ARE WE CHANGING?

As an insider you may or may not be informed as to why change is understood to be needed. Senior management may assume that you know from your experience that change is needed, i.e. there are less customers in the shop. Knowing why change is being embarked on is a critical element of you and your colleagues' perception and assessment of and responses to the changes.

WHERE ARE WE HEADED?

Where are the changes taking us? What is the vision of the future? Such a picture of a desired future is critical as it helps provide focus and energy because it describes the desires for the future in a positive light and provides meaning for employees' response. As an insider you and your work colleagues may not be informed about the positive vision of the desired future state of the organization and this lack of information may contribute to how the change is assessed and the kinds of responses generated.

WHAT IS NEEDED TO CHANGE TO GET THERE?

Because the present situation is being assessed in the light of the desired future, assessment of what needs changing and what does not may be controversial and divisive. For you as the insider, understanding or not the choices of what is to change is grounded in your perception and assessment of the change. Your work colleagues may or may not understand or agree what needs to change and you may observe denying and dodging as groups seek to protect their turf.

HOW DO WE WORK THROUGH THE TRANSITION?

The transition state between the present and the future is typically a difficult time because the past is found to be defective and no longer tenable and the new state has not yet come into being. So, in essence, the transition state is somewhat particular, as the old has gone and the new has not yet been realized, and so needs to be seen and managed as such. It is a messy time and state of affairs, where unanticipated events interrupt the formalized plan or its schedule. As the insider, you may be noticing how the messiness of being in the in-between state and the often accompanying stress and conflict are being handled.

REINFORCING AND SUSTAINING THE CHANGE

Reinforcement involves consolidation so that the changes are embedded in operational practice. Sustaining is a longer-term focus than reinforcement or consolidation as it attends to keeping the momentum going. As an insider you may be attentive to whether there are reinforcement mechanisms being used or if you're being left to your own devices and in effect slipping back into the old ways of doing things.

INTERLEVEL DYNAMICS OF ORGANIZATIONAL CHANGE

The movement through the five steps involves sensitivity to process – how information is shared and heard, how decisions are made, how vision is articulated, where interventions are judged to be necessary or desired and so on, so that the change is made effectively. It also involves interlevel dynamics as information is gathered and processed, decisions are made, their consequences are followed through by a complex interaction of individuals, individuals in teams and working groups and between teams.

As described in Chapter 5, what happens at one level has an impact on each of the others. So, for example, a recession may lead to a retrenchment of services and staff numbers. This affects the organization's resource allocation across its departments and services, leading to a change in the work of teams who may have fewer members and an increased workload, and result in individuals becoming stressed and alienated from their professional work. If a team is working well, that contributes positively to the motivation and participation of the individual members; the reverse is also true. The work of one team affects the work of others. So each level is systemically linked to each of the others and events at one level are both cause and effect of events at other levels.

The process of organizational change is itself an interlevel process. A change process has to begin somewhere and typically it begins with an individual, though not exclusively at the top. That individual may deny and dodge before deciding to take action, that is to move to doing. For the change agenda to progress, that individual has to take it to a team and that team needs to adopt the need for change. The team may engage in denying and dodging before it moves to doing. When a management team adopts the need for change and begins to act, it has then to win over other teams in the system. Other teams may engage in denying and dodging before they move to doing. Of course, at any point denying or dodging may prevail and then the change does not go any further, but rather returns to whomever was at the doing stage. That individual or team may then revert to dodging or if committed to doing may have to adopt a different approach or strategy to get beyond the dodging stage of the others.

Each of these movements – from individual to team to other teams – is an iterative process. In other words, when the team adopts an individual's position, that adoption reinforces the individual. When other teams adopt a particular team's position, that reinforces that team, and, of course, when customers adopt a new product or service, that reinforces the organization. The process of defining the future involves interlevel dynamics.

If the vision comes from the chief executive, then there are interlevel dynamics from that individual to the senior management group and then to the other teams and on to the organization. So the iteration of issue presentation, reaction and response ebbs and flows from individual to individual, team to team and so on. The process of designing the vision of the future involves interlevel dynamics. Interlevel dynamics are pivotal to the processes of the transition state as individuals and teams address the implications and implementation of the change agenda. As the change agenda affects the work of individuals in what they do and how they do it, individual commitment is essential. As the change agenda affects the work of the permanent teams and typically requires the creation of new teams and work in temporary committees or project groups, team dynamics are critical to the change process. In a similar vein, the change agenda involves the interface of multiple teams with respect to information sharing, problem identification and resolution, resource allocation and collective bargaining, and inter-team dynamics can enable or hinder the successful management of the change process.

The clinical perspective in being attentive to the above processes provides a rich treasury of questions to be pursued. You may wonder about denials of the need for change or expressions of dodging. You may notice how assessment of the present creates defensiveness in individuals, teams and between teams where there are tendencies to attempt to shift blame for change problems from one team onto another. You may be wondering what is going on when people close ranks and identify with their own team and exclude engagement with other teams.

Take a reflective pause to map the process of a change in your organization.

REFLECTIVE PAUSE

Reflect on a change in your organization:

- Why did the organization need to (or say it needed to) change?
- Was there a sense of a desired future?
- Was there a plan for change that was clearly linked to the stated desired future?
- How was the uncertainty of the transition state managed?
- Were there reinforcing mechanisms?
- What evidence do you have for your experience and insights into each of the above?
- Can you inquire into the change from the different perspectives, especially from your colleagues' perspectives (key insider knowledge)?
- What individual/team/interdepartmental group/organizational change is evident in your case?

- Do phases and levels provide any insight into what stage the change is at and help you understand who is doing what?
- What is your insight into what happened/might happen next?

STRATEGIC FOCI AND LARGE SYSTEM CHANGE

In the previous chapter, I explored strategic processes through the framework of the five strategic foci. From this chapter you can see that the enactment of the strategic foci links integrally to the interlevel dynamics of intentional strategic change as the activities of large system change are essential to the implementation of a change in strategy. For example, a strategic imperative for change may come from doing corporate analysis or from assessing corporate outcomes. The framing of a new corporate picture or corporate words is integrally linked to articulating a desired future and may, in effect, open up a second-order change. Enactment of a second-order change in strategy or a first-order improvement initiative in corporate actions and the engagement in evaluating corporate outcomes are, as we have seen above, complex interlevel activities. Implementation of a change in strategy involves moving from a perceived need for change from corporate analysis or from assessing corporate outcomes, through articulating an envisioned future, through assessing the present to determine what needs to change and getting to the envisioned future by implementing change and managing the transition.

CONCLUSIONS

This chapter has taken up the processes of the interlevel dynamics of organizational learning and change. At the heart of both processes is how information is received into an organization, processed and transformed into outputs. All learning and change involve acquiring, interpreting and applying information. How that is done reflects the health of the system. Hence the emphasis in this chapter is on process, particularly interlevel processes of learning and change. The clinical perspective of insider inquiry invites you to be attentive to how the health of the system is expressed in how information is received into an organization, is processed and is transformed into outputs.

8

CONCLUSIONS

Learning to bring an attitude of inquiry to experience is at the heart of the educational process. As you experience processes in organizations, you see things happening and you hear what is said. How do you understand them? And then what judgements do you make about them? So you need to learn to be attentive to what is happening, ask yourself relevant questions, questions that are based on wanting to understand what is going on. You try to keep an open mind as to what events might mean until you have gathered your evidence and verified it by judgement. Learning to develop an inquiring attentiveness to organizational processes which occur around us is a core skill for us to learn. You can learn to observe yourself and learn to understand yourselves as a questioner. Learning a method of attending to cognitional processes is accessible to us as it is grounded, not in any thesis or grand theory, but in the recognizable operations of human inquiry.

As Coghlan and Graham Cagney explore, no matter which way one approaches it, undergraduate students may find insider inquiry difficult and troublesome for several reasons. One reason is that their academic learning to date has been primarily propositional rather than practical. They have studied theories, concepts and frameworks and applied them to paper-based cases, which typically tend to be constructed on a discipline basis. Engaging with how these theories are enacted in practice involves an ability to integrate fields of study, which hitherto in the students' experience may not have been integrated. A second reason is that learning from the closeness of direct experience where meanings are socially constructed requires students to be skilled both in understanding what is taking place in the environment around them and in grasping their own meaning-making processes. This is learning that is not amenable to adopting frameworks and simple rules blindly. Indeed, it can only be learned by engaging in it. It is paramount to have a method that students can learn and that enables them to practise this 'multisensory holistic immersion' and 'messy iterative groping' within course constraints.

In this book I have explored how insider inquiry skill, as a core skill for undergraduate business students, is engaged in through a general empirical method that mirrors the operations of human knowing. The foundation of the book is that insider inquiry is an important area of learning for students who are in transition from college life to the world of working in organizations. In Evered and Louis's terms such inquiry is engaged in by 'multisensory holistic immersion' and 'messy, iterative groping' in what Schon termed the 'swampy lowlands'. The insider inquiry approach contrasts with the outsider observer approach of the case study method. Engaging in insider inquiry demands a reversal of academic learning approaches, whereby the students begin from experience rather than from theory. Learning from the closeness of direct experience where meanings are socially constructed requires students to be skilled in both understanding what is taking place in the environment around them and in grasping their own meaning-making processes. This is learning that is not amenable simply to adopting frameworks and simplistic rules, but rather by direct engagement and reflection on that engagement through questioning experience in the light of relevant theory. In other words the enactment of the learning formula $L = P + Q$, through being attentive to what is going on around you, being intelligent in your understanding, being reasonable in your judgements and being responsible for your actions.

Appendix 1

KEEPING A LEARNING JOURNAL

A learning journal is a record of your efforts to puzzle through events, thoughts and feelings about a particular aspect of life close to when these events take place. It reflects your own effort to capture your learning as it unfolds over time. It can record anything and in any way in relation to the issues under consideration. There are many reasons for keeping a journal. You may want to capture an experience before you forget it, to explore your feelings or to make sense of what you are puzzling over. Most times you write for yourself; other times you are required to write for others such as when prescribed in a course.

With respect to the context where journal keeping is prescribed in a course, journal writing is intimately linked to learning through how it enhances reflection and reflective practice. Reflection is the means by which experience is turned into learning through exploring experiences so as to learn from them. Writing a learning journal means puzzling through what is happening at work and in your life. A learning journal is like a diary but it is oriented towards learning and thus towards deliberative thought and analysis related to practice, and so it is a vehicle for reflection. In terms of the learning formula $L = P + Q$, your journal is your personal record of how your learning (L) is emerging from your subjecting espoused theory (P) to questioning (Q) from your experience. It is expected that your journal is private and confidential, for your eyes only, though in a course setting your supervisor may read it and is expected to keep its contents confidential. The Reflective Pauses dotted throughout the chapters are another source of journal entries.

There are several purposes of keeping a learning journal. The main purpose is to deepen the quality of your learning through critical thinking and by developing a questioning attitude. Accordingly, a second purpose is to enable you to understand and increase participation and ownership of your own learning process, rather than being dependent on a textbook or a lecture. Essentially a journal captures

1   what took place on a particular occasion (what you and others said and did)
2   what you thought and felt about what happened and probably didn't say at the time
3   what your reflection is on both of the above.

In terms of the *general empirical method* introduced in Chapter 2, what a learning journal seeks to capture is how you try to:

- be *attentive* to what is going on around you
- be *intelligent* in your understanding
- be *reasonable* in your judgements
- be *responsible* for your actions.

While journals may be highly structured or unstructured, in the context of keeping a learning journal in a course, it is useful to have some structure so as to keep track of your learning and so that your lecturer may be able to evaluate it. A useful format might be:

1   Recount an incident – who said and did what, what you thought and felt.
2   What questions arise for you from that incident?
3   What insights have you into that incident? About the situation? About you?
4   Can you test or have you tested those insights? Question your own thinking.
5   Then/now what?

It is important that journal entries are linked to one another so that your reflection on a particular incident finds echoes in your reflection on other and later incidents, where you might show how you learned from an earlier incident or that you haven't and how that sets up a further question and inquiry. A learning journal maps reflection over time as well as at a particular time, hence dating your entries enables you to view developments over time.

Appendix 2

WRITING A REFLECTIVE ESSAY

Writing a reflective essay is different from writing a traditional essay. A reflective essay aims at showing how you have turned experience into learning. As such learning is emergent rather than planned and your paper needs to provide evidence of how your reflection on events and your own thinking have changed you in some way. Your reflective essay needs to show how the learning formula, $L = P + Q$, has happened for you, that you demonstrate your learning about your organization and your own thinking through a clinical approach. As Chapter 2 introduced, the clinical approach involves building theory and empirical knowledge: in-depth observation of crucial cases of learning and change, studying the effects of interventions and focusing on the characteristic of systems that are difficult to explain. This clinical approach gives focus to the learning formula, $L=P+Q$, as it sharpens the questioning of insider experience and engages that questioning with knowledge of organizational theory and behaviour so as to generate learning.

Essentially a reflective essay captures your learning from reflecting on a situation or a series of events. So it is more than simply describing what took place. Merely describing what happened does not constitute reflective thinking. Reflective thinking requires showing how you have thought about what took place and how you have thought about your thinking about it. In other words your reflective essay captures the inner and outer arcs of attention and your use of the general empirical method which takes you from experience to understanding to testing that understanding to judgement. In moving through the general empirical method the challenge is to show evidence of your learning from the searching questions that you have been asking. Use useful tools that you have learned, such as the JOHARI Window, Transactional Analysis, the Ladder of Inference, taking facts as hypotheses or the double-column technique. Be wary of making untested inferences or attributions.

Examples of questions that may help your critical thinking are:

- What assumptions were you making at the outset? Did you challenge them and then were they confirmed or disconfirmed?
- What surprised, annoyed ... you most?
- Does your reasoning process follow the general empirical method and show how attentive you were to your experience, how your understanding is intelligent and your judgements are reasonable?
- Are there alternative explanations or conclusions other than yours? How have you considered them?
- What have you learned about yourself – how you think, how you relate?
- What might you do differently if similar situations occur?

The core source of your reflective essay is likely to be your learning journal where, in the mode of the clinical approach, you have captured the exploration of your thinking about incidents in the organization and about your thinking about your thinking. The quality of your journal keeping contributes to what you can draw on for a reflective essay, particularly if you are writing about incidents that took place some time ago. Parallel to drawing on your journal is how you draw on what you have read (the P of the learning formula). Your reading will have informed your understanding and challenged your thinking (the Q of the learning formula). Inquiring into your own thinking also provides the challenge to confront any disparity between your thinking in the past when events took place and current hindsight as you write your paper now.

While there is no standardized format for reflective essays, it is useful to have some structure so as to be able to articulate your learning so that your lecturer may be able to evaluate it. A useful format might be:

- Summarize a series of incidents – who said and did what, what you thought and felt over the series of events. What P are you drawing on?
- What question arises for you from those incidents? How is P challenged?
- What insights have you into those incidents? About the situation? About you?
- Have you tested those insights? What further reading (P) has helped you test them and consolidate or challenge your insights? How have you been critical of your own thinking about these events?
- What are the overall judgements that you are making after multiple experiences, insights and judgements over the time of your inquiry. What's your theory of your organization that you have verified empirically?
- Show *how* you have learned as well as *what* you have learned.

Appendix 3

GUIDING AND SUPERVISING INSIDER INQUIRY

This appendix is directed to supervisors, mentors and those who guide students engaging in insider inquiry. The general empirical method introduced in Chapter 2 and followed through the book is a useful framework for supervisors and mentors to follow and it stays consistent with what the student are attempting. The students are invited to describe their experiences and their questions arising from those experiences, name their insights and then verify them. The general empirical method is to: be attentive to experience, be intelligent in understanding and be reasonable in affirming judgements. Supervisors may support their students to describe their experiences, to show how their understanding and their judgements are intelligent and how their articulated learning is reasonable.

Utilizing the work of Edgar Schein who has written extensively on how to be helpful, which, of course, is the intention of the supervisor or mentor, the following approach is suggested. Schein describes several types of inquiry and frames a typology of interventions (see Table 1). His first category is what he calls *pure inquiry*. This is where supervisors and mentors listen carefully and neutrally to the stories that the students describe and prompt the elicitation and exploration of the story of what is taking place. Examples of pure inquiry interventions are: Tell me what happened? Who said what to whom? Then what happened? What did you do? Questions such as these enable the students to relate their experience and allow them to feel ownership of their stories' issues and experience the facilitative role of the supervisor. It would be expected that these experiences are recorded in the students' learning journals.

The second type of inquiry is what Schein calls *diagnostic inquiry*, in which supervisors begin to guide the students' thinking process. Examples of helpful questions in this mode are: What do you think was going on in this episode? How did you feel about that? Is there anything you've read that helps you make sense of what took place?

The third type of inquiry is what Schein calls *confrontive inquiry*. This is where supervisors, by sharing their own ideas, challenge the students to think from an alternative

APPENDIX 3

Table 1 Intervention Typology

Task	Intervention	Useful Questions
Uncovering Experience	*Pure Inquiry*	Tell me what happened? Who said what to whom? Then what happened? What did you do?
Probing for Insight	*Diagnostic Inquiry*	What do you think was going on in this episode? How did you feel about that? Is there anything you've read that helps you make sense of what took place?
Aiming for Judgement	*Confrontive*	Have you considered ... as an alternative interpretation? Look up X.

perspective. Here supervisors may direct the students to other viewpoints and may suggest new or alternative readings.

Through pure, diagnostic and confrontive inquiry, supervisors and mentors engage with the students to draw out their experience, articulate their insights and verify their judgements. They are helping the students attend to their experience, have insights into those experiences, make judgements as to whether the insights fit the evidence. The conversations between supervisors and students enable the students to tell the stories of their insider experiences (through pure inquiry), to articulate their insights and interpretations (through diagnostic inquiry) and to frame these insights as reasonable judgements and formulate their learning (through confrontive inquiry). With supervisors' and mentors' interventions in harmony with how the students are engaging with their insider inquiry the learning may be enhanced.

Appendix 4

RESEARCHING FROM THE INSIDE

This appendix is directed towards readers whose insider inquiry is undertaken as more formalized research, for a dissertation, for example. This appendix locates inquiry from the inside in a philosophy of social science that seeks to understand meaning and introduces some basic tenets of insider research.

The history of the philosophy of social science demonstrates debates about a distinction between approaches that pursue explanation and those that pursue understanding. The former emulates the natural sciences and works with grounding research in comparable standards of evidence prediction and inference and leads to the empiricist tradition of research. The latter, critical of the former's ability to deal with human meaning, seeks to emphasize the interpretation of human meaning in the science of human organization and action and leads to the interpretive tradition of research. For example, the symbolic interactionist approach, found in Goffman's work explored in Chapter 1, reflects the social nature of meaning and how it is constructed and maintained through social interaction. Hollis notes that there are two stories to tell about the social world and how it works. One starts as the insider's or agent's story about what social life means and the other as an outsider's or spectator's story about the causes of social behaviour and action.

Insider inquiry as more formalized research typically finds its home in the philosophy of social science that purses understanding. It values and addresses the experience of being a participant and it builds up insider knowledge. The challenge for insider researchers is to use their experience, intelligence and reason in order to come to know the mixture of experience, understanding, judgements and actions in their organizational setting and to show how they are providing a reasonable account of the available evidence.

In a seminal article, Evered and Louis distinguish between 'inquiry from the inside' and 'inquiry from the outside'. 'Inquiry from the outside' refers to traditional science where the researchers' relationship to the setting is detached and neutral. Typically researchers act as onlookers, and they apply a priori categories to create universal, context free knowledge. The basis for validity is measurement and logic. In contrast, 'inquiry from the inside' involves researchers as actors, immersed in local situations generating contextually embedded knowledge that emerges from experience. Alvesson uses the term 'self-ethnography' to describe insider research in which the researcher-author describes a cultural setting to which he/she has a 'natural access', is an active participant and is more or less on equal terms with other participants. The researcher then works and/or lives in the setting and uses the experiences, knowledge and access to empirical material for research purposes. He argues that 'observing participant' is a better term to use than 'participant observer'. Participation comes first and is only occasionally complemented with observation in a research-focus sense.

Insider inquiry works from direct personal experience. Evered and Louis refer to their method of insider inquiry as 'multisensory holistic immersion' and as 'messy, iterative groping', which they contrast with procedures of forming and testing explicit hypotheses associated with the scientific method. As insiders listen to what people say, observe what people do and question the outcomes of deliberate and spontaneous action, intended and unintended, they learn to 'decipher the blooming, buzzing confusion' around them.

The general empirical method introduced in Chapter 2 provides a rigorous method that enables inquiry into experience and self-reflectiveness on how one is constructing interpretations. Insider researchers use their own experience, intelligence and reason in order to come to know the behaviour of the members of the organization under study. Such a critically reflective approach enables insider researchers to articulate tacit knowledge which has become deeply segmented due to socialization in an organizational system, and reframe it as theoretical knowledge. Reflexivity is the concept used in the social sciences to explore and deal with the relationship between the researcher and the object of research.

For some insider researchers insider inquiry may be grounded in an approach that seeks not only to understand their own organization but also to change it. This approach is termed action research and involves the deliberate construction, planning, enactment and evaluation of cycles of action and reflection. Such insider action research requires explicit attention to the politics of change in building collaborative relations with key stakeholders and commitment to the change. Selection of an insider action research approach tends to be adopted by those who are in a managerial position to enact change in their own organization and who act as scholar-practitioners in integrating their practice with research.

REFERENCES AND SUGGESTED READING

INTRODUCTION

Costley, C. and Armsby, P. (2007) 'Methodologies for undergraduates doing practitioner investigations at work', *Journal of Workplace Learning*, 19 (3): 131–145.

Fineman, S., Gabriel, Y. and Sims, D. (2010) *Organizing and Organizations*, 4th edn. London: SAGE.

Schein, E.H. (1996) 'Kurt Lewin's change theory in the field and in the classroom: notes toward a model of managed learning', *Systems Practice*, 9 (1): 27–47.

CHAPTER 1

Argyris, C. (2010) *Organizational Traps*. New York: Oxford University Press.

Bennis, W., Van Maanen, J., Schein, E.H. and Steele, F. (1979) *Essays in Interpersonal Dynamics*. Homewood, IL: Dorsey Press.

Bolman, L.G. and Deal, T.E. (2013) *Reframing Organizations: Artistry, Choice, and Leadership*. San Francisco: Jossey-Bass.

Campbell, D. (2000) *The Socially Constructed Organization*. London: Karnac.

Goffman, E. (1975) *The Presentation of Self in Everyday Life*. London: Penguin.

Hatch, M.J. and Cunliffe, A. (2013) *Organization Theory*, 3rd edn. Oxford: Oxford University Press.

Mike, B. (2014) 'Footprints in the sand: Edgar Schein', *Organizational Dynamics*, 43: 321–328.

Morgan, G. (1985) *Images of Organization*. Thousand Oaks, CA: SAGE.

Schein, E.H. (2009) *The Corporate Culture Survival Guide*, 2nd edn. San Francisco: Jossey-Bass.

CHAPTER 2

Argyris, C. (2010) *Organizational Traps*. New York: Oxford University Press.

Burns, D. (2000) *Feeling Good*. Harper: New York.

Evered, R. and Louis, M.R. (1981) 'Alternative perspectives in the organisational sciences: "Inquiry from the inside" and "inquiry from the outside"', *Academy of Management Review*, 6: 385–395.

Flanagan, J. (1997) *Quest for Self-Understanding*. Toronto: Toronto University Press.

Kahneman, D. (2011) *Thinking Fast and Slow*. New York: Penguin.

Lonergan, B.J. (1992) *The Collected Works of Bernard Lonergan*, Vol. 3. *Insight: An Essay in Human Understanding*, ed. F. Crowe and R. Doran. Toronto: University of Toronto Press (original publication, London: Longmans, 1957).

Marshall, J. (1999) 'Living life as inquiry', *Systemic Practice and Action Research*, 12: 155–171.

Moon, J. (2008) *Critical Thinking*. London: Routledge.

Revans, R. (2011) *ABC of Action Learning*. Farnham: Gower

Schein, E.H. (1997) 'Organizational learning: what is new?' In M.A. Rahim, R.T. Golembiewski and L.E. Pate (eds), *Current Topics in Management*, Vol. 2. Greenwich, CT: JAI Press, pp. 11–26.

Schon, D.A. (2004) 'Knowing-in-action: the new scholarship requires a new epistemology'. In B. Cooke and J. Wolfram-Cox (eds), *Fundamentals of Action Research*, Vol. III. London: SAGE, pp. 377–394.

CHAPTER 3

Berne, E. (2010) *Games People Play*. Harmondsworth: Penguin.

Berne, E. (1975) *What Do You Do After You Say Hello?* London: Corgi.

Harris, T. (2012) *I'm OK. You're OK*. London: Arrow.

James, M. and Jongeward, D. (1976) *Everybody Wins: Transactional Analysis Applied to Organizations*. Reading, MA: Addison-Wesley.

Schein, E.H. (2013) *Humble Inquiry: The Gentle Art of Asking Instead of Telling*. San Francisco: Berrett-Koehler.

Stewart, I. and Joines, V. (2012) *TA Today: A New Introduction to Transactional Analysis*, 2nd edn. Derby: Lifespace.

CHAPTER 4

Argyris, C. (2010) *Organizational Traps*. New York: Oxford University Press.

Hirschhorn, L. (1988) *The Workplace Within*. Cambridge, MA: MIT Press.

Marshak, R. (2006) *Covert Processes at Work*. San Francisco: Berrett-Kohler.

CHAPTER 5

Ashforth, B. and Lee, R., (1990) 'Defensive behavior in organizations: a preliminary model', *Human Relations*, 43 (7): 621–648.

Bento, R. (1994) 'When the show must go on: disenfranchised grief in organizations', *Journal of Managerial Psychology*, 9 (6): 35–44.

Coghlan, D., Rashford, N.S. and Neiva de Figueiredo, J. (2016) *Organizational Change and Strategy: An Interlevel Dynamics Approach*, 2nd edn. Abingdon: Routledge.

Fineman, S. (1993) *Emotion in Organizations*. London: SAGE.

Greiner, L. (1972) 'Evolution and revolution as organizations grow', *Harvard Business Review*, July/August.

Mann, S. (1997) 'Emotional labour in organizations', *Leadership and Organization Development Journal*, 18 (1): 4–12.

Michelson, G. and Mouly, S. (2000) 'Rumour and gossip in organizations: a conceptual study', *Management Decision*, 38 (5): 339–346.

Mishra, J. (1990) 'Managing the grapevine', *Public Personnel Management*, 19 (2): 213–228

Merry, U. and Brown, G. (1987) *The Neurotic Behavior of Organizations*. Cleveland, OH: Gestalt Institute of Cleveland Press.

Morris, J.A. and Feldman, D.C. (1996) 'The dimensions, antecedents and consequences of emotional labour', *Academy of Management Review*, 21 (4): 986–1010.

Palmer, B. and McCaughan, N. (1994) *Systems Thinking for Harassed Managers*. London: Karnac.

Parment, A. (2012) *Generation Y in Consumer and Labour Markets*. Abingdon: Routledge.

Parrott, G.S. and Smith R.H. (1993) 'Distinguishing the experiences of envy and jealousy', *Journal of Personality and Social Psychology*, 64: 906–920.

Rothlin, P. and Werder, P. (2008) *Boreout! Overcoming Workplace Demotivation*. London: Kogan Page.

Schein, E.H. (1978) *Career Dynamics*. Reading, MA: Addison-Wesley.

Schein, E.H. (2004) 'Learning when and how to lie: a neglected aspect of organizational and occupational socialization', *Human Relations*, 17 (3): 259–273.

Senge, P. (1990) *The Fifth Discipline*. New York: Doubleday.

Senge, P., Roberts, C., Ross, R., Smith, B. and Kleiner, A. (1994) *The Fifth Discipline Fieldbook*. London: Nicholas Brealey.

Stapley, L. (2006) *Individuals, Groups and Organizations Beneath the Surface*. London: Karnac.

Waddington, K. (2013) *Gossip and Organizations*. Abingdon: Routledge.

CHAPTER 6

Argyris, C. (1985) *Strategy, Change and Defensive Routines*. Boston: Pitman.

Argyris, C. and Schon, D. (1996) *Organizational Learning II*. Reading, MA: Addison-Wesley.

Bolman, L.G. and Deal, T.E. (2013) *Reframing Organizations: Artistry, Choice, and Leadership*, 5th edn. San Francisco: Jossey-Bass.

Coghlan, D. and Rashford, N.S. and Neiva de Figueiredo, J. (2016) *Organizational Change and Strategy: An Interlevel Dynamics Approach*, 2nd edn. Abingdon: Routledge.

Fisher, D., Rooke, D. and Torbert, W.R. (2000) *Personal and Organizational Transformations through Action Inquiry*. Boston: Edge/Work Press.

Mintzberg, H. (1992) 'Five Ps for strategy'. In H. Mintzberg and J.B. Quinn (eds), *The Strategy Process*. Englewood Cliffs, NJ: Prentice-Hall International Editions, pp. 12–19.

Torbert, W.R. and Associates (2004) *Action Inquiry*. San Francisco: Berrett-Koehler.

CHAPTER 7

Argyris, C. (1990) *Overcoming Organizational Defenses*. Boston, MA: Allyn & Bacon.

Argyris, C. and Schon, D. (1996) *Organizational Learning II*. Reading, MA: Addison-Wesley.

Beckhard, R. and Harris, R. (1987) *Organizational Transitions: Managing Complex Change*, 2nd edn. Reading, MA: Addison-Wesley.

Coghlan, D. and Rashford, N.S. and Neiva de Figueiredo, J. (2016) *Organizational Change and Strategy: An Interlevel Dynamics Approach*, 2nd edn. Abingdon: Routledge.

Crossan, M., Lane, H. and White, R. (1999) 'An organizational learning framework: from intuiting to institution', *Academy of Management Review*, 24 (3): 522–537.

Schein, E.H. (2009) *The Corporate Culture Survival Guide*, 2nd edn. San Francisco: Jossey-Bass.

CHAPTER 8

Coghlan, D. and Graham Cagney, A. (2013) '"Multisensory holistic immersion": a method of insider inquiry as a threshold concept', *Journal of Learning Development in Higher Education*, Issue 5.

Dewey, J. (1938) *Experience and Education*. New York: Macmillan.

Evered, R. and Louis, M.R. (1981) 'Alternative perspectives in the organizational sciences: "Inquiry from the inside" and "inquiry from the outside"', *Academy of Management Review*, 6: 385–395.

APPENDIX 1

Basset, S. (2013) *The Reflective Journal*. London: Palgrave.

Bolton, G. (2005) *Reflective Practice*. London: SAGE.

Moon, J. (1999) *Learning Journals*. London: Kogan Page.

APPENDIX 2

Cunliffe, A.L. (2009) 'Reflexivity, learning and reflexive practice'. In S. Armstrong and C. Fukami (eds), *Handbook in Management Learning, Education and Development*. London: SAGE, pp. 405–418.

APPENDIX 3

Coghlan, D. (2009) 'Toward a philosophy of clinical inquiry/research', *Journal of Applied Behavioral Science*, 45 (1): 106–121.

Schein, E.H. (2009) *Helping*. San Francisco: Berrett-Koehler.

Schein, E.H. (2013) *Humble Inquiry: The Gentle Art of Asking Instead of Telling*. San Francisco: Berrett-Koehler.

APPENDIX 4

Adler, P.A. and Adler, P. (1987) *Membership Roles in Field Research*. Thousand Oaks, CA: SAGE.

Alvesson, M. (2003) 'Methodology for close up studies: struggling with closeness and closure', *Higher Education*, 46: 167–193.

Brannick, T. and Coghlan, D. (2007) 'In defense of being "native": the case for insider academic research', *Organization Research Methods*, 10 (1): 59–74.

Coghlan, D. (2013) 'Messy, iterative groping in the swampy lowlands: the challenges of inside scholar-practitioner inquiry'. In A.B. (Rami) Shani, W.A. Pasmore and R.W. Woodman (eds), *Research in Organization Change and Development*, Vol. 21. Brinkley: Emerald, pp. 121–147.

Coghlan, D. and Brannick, T. (2014) *Doing Action Research in Your Own Organization*, 4th edn. London: SAGE.

Cunliffe, A. (2003) 'Reflexive enquiry in organizational research', *Human Relations*, 56: 987–1003.

Evered, R. and Louis, M.R. (1981) 'Alternative perspectives in the organizational sciences: "Inquiry from the inside" and "inquiry from the outside"', *Academy of Management Review*, 6: 385–395.

Hollis, M. (2002) *The Philosophy of Social Science*, revised and updated edn. Cambridge: Cambridge University Press.

Schein, E.H (1987) *The Clinical Perspective in Fieldwork*. Thousand Oaks, CA: SAGE.

INDEX

INDEX